On Lingering and Literature

Lingering and its decried equivalents, such as dawdling, idling, loafing, or lolling about, are both shunned and coveted in our culture where time is money and where there is never quite enough of either. Is lingering lazy? Is it childish? Boring? Do poets linger? (Is that why poetry is boring?) Is it therapeutic? Should we linger more? Less? What happens when we linger? Harold Schweizer here examines an experience of time that, though common, usually passes unnoticed.

Drawing on a wide range of philosophic and literary texts and examples, *On Lingering and Literature* exemplifies in its style and accessible argumentation the new genre of post-criticism, and aims to reward anyone interested in slow reading, daydreaming, or resisting our culture of speed and consumption.

Harold Schweizer is Professor Emeritus of English at Bucknell University, USA, where he taught poetry, literary theory, and Holocaust and trauma studies. Recipient of two awards for excellence in teaching, he is a widely published poet and literary critic. His most recent books are *On Waiting*; *Rarity and the Poetic*; and the poetry volumes *The Book of Stones and Angels*, *Miriam's Book*, and *The Genealogy of Elevators*.

Routledge Focus on Literature

The Quarrel Between Poetry and Philosophy
Perspectives Across the Humanities
John Burns, Matthew Caleb Flamm, William Gahan, and Stephanie Quinn

Nineteenth-Century Italian Women Writers and the Woman Question
The Case of Neera
Catherine Ramsey-Portolano

Dialogue in the Digital Age
Why it Matters How We Read and What We Say
Patrick Grant

On Lingering and Literature
Harold Schweizer

The Rise of the Australian Neurohumanities
Conversations Between Neurocognitive Research and Australian Literature
Edited by Jean-François Vernay

Neo-Georgian Fiction
Re-imagining the Eighteenth Century in the Contemporary Historical Novel
Edited by Jakub Lipski and Joanna Maciulewicz

For more information about this series, please visit: https://www.routledge.com/Routledge-Focus-on-Literature/book-series/RFLT

On Lingering and Literature

Harold Schweizer

LONDON AND NEW YORK

First published
by Routledge
2 Park Square, Milton Park, Abingdon, Oxon OX14 4RN
and by Routledge
52 Vanderbilt Avenue, New York, NY 10017

Routledge is an imprint of the Taylor & Francis Group, an informa business

© 2021 Harold Schweizer

The right of Harold Schweizer to be identified as author of this work has been asserted by him in accordance with sections 77 and 78 of the Copyright, Designs and Patents Act 1988.

All rights reserved. No part of this book may be reprinted or reproduced or utilised in any form or by any electronic, mechanical, or other means, now known or hereafter invented, including photocopying and recording, or in any information storage or retrieval system, without permission in writing from the publishers.

Trademark notice: Product or corporate names may be trademarks or registered trademarks, and are used only for identification and explanation without intent to infringe.

British Library Cataloguing-in-Publication Data
A catalogue record for this book is available from the British Library

Library of Congress Cataloging-in-Publication Data
Names: Schweizer, Harold, 1950- author.
Title: On lingering and literature / Harold Schweizer.
Description: Abingdon, Oxdon; New York, NY : Routledge, 2021. | Includes bibliographical references and index.
Identifiers: LCCN 2020044670 | ISBN 9780367740375 (hardback) | ISBN 9781003155850 (ebook)
Subjects: LCSH: Lingering (Philosophy) in literature. | Time perception in literature.
Classification: LCC PN56.L537 S39 2021 | DDC 809/.9384–dc23
LC record available at https://lccn.loc.gov/2020044670

ISBN: 978-0-367-74037-5 (hbk)
ISBN: 978-0-367-74059-7 (pbk)
ISBN: 978-1-003-15585-0 (ebk)

Typeset in Times New Roman
by Taylor & Francis Books

Every effort has been made to contact copyright-holders. Please advise the publisher of any errors or omissions, and these will be corrected in subsequent editions.

For Saundra Kay

Contents

	Preface	viii
1	A moment, please	1
2	The temporality of the beautiful	13
3	The economics of waiting	20
4	The poet's idleness	28
5	The ecstasy of slowness	34
6	The temporality of Whitman's grass	46
7	The slowness of looking	53
8	Virginia Woolf's indescribable pause	61
9	Proustian interludes	75
10	The weight of Sebald's time	93
11	Instead of concluding: Stopping	108
	Bibliography	115
	Index	120

Preface

This book begins in my childhood, in my enchanted lingering on the granite steps of our small front yard, the rhythm of the names of the Alpine mountains in my ears, *Mürtschenstock, Fronalpstock, Rautispitz, Vrenelisgärtli*, the smell of pine trees and lavender from the garden. It begins on the day when I heard the teacher's voice far away while the sun silvered the tips of the high grass outside the windows, while the wind made the meadow move like water. "[T]he whole experience comes back to me after the lapse of forty and more years," Walt Whitman recalls, "the soothing rustle of the waves, and the saline smell—boyhood's times, the clam-digging, barefoot, and with trowsers roll'd up—hauling down the creek—the perfume of the sedge-meadows...."[1] Or here is the last stanza from William Saphire's "Childhood Memories":

> My memory is a sigh
> of swallows swinging
> through a slow dormant summer
> to a timid line on the horizon.[2]

Who does not remember such charmed eternities of childhood? "These times without a clock," French philosopher Gaston Bachelard writes, "are still within us."[3] This is a book about such times. It is about what we do when we do nothing.

It is not easy to say what nothing is; nor is it easy to do nothing. Not even the authors of Genesis could imagine Adam and Eve doing nothing. In Milton's paradise we find them resting from the "toil / Of their sweet gard'ning labor"[4] in accord with the Biblical injunction that they "dress it and keep it" (2:15). Both the author of Genesis and the poet John Milton seem to insist that even in paradise we perforce must be doing something. Do "these times without a clock" exist if they don't exist even in the garden of Eden? Do we recall such times merely in our memories of childhood—of the sun silvering the tips of the high grass, of swallows swinging through a slow, dormant summer?

On the occasion of their meeting on April 6, 1922, the eminent philosopher Henri Bergson proposed to Albert Einstein that there exists a time in one's life that we experience "prior to all physics." "Prior to all physics" would be prior to all clocks and measurements; it implies precisely the kind of paradisical childhood time that I mentioned above. To the famous physicist, however, such experiences remained merely subjective: "there is no philosopher's time," Einstein is said to have replied.[5] This book, then, builds its case on an impossible philosopher's time, an implausible time, an untimely time that has to no one's surprise acquired a wholly dubious reputation. For what do we do when we do nothing? What is it that we do when we merely linger? If Adam and Eve had only attended to their sweet gard'ning labor they would not have succumbed to the serpent's temptation.

Lingering and its decried equivalents, such as dawdling, idling, loafing, or lolling about, are both shunned and coveted in our culture where time is money and where there is never quite enough of either. Is lingering lazy? Is it childish? Sinful? Boring? Do poets linger? (Is that why poetry is boring?) Is it therapeutic? Do the rich linger and the poor wait? Should we linger more? Less? What happens when we linger? These are some of the questions I consider here. I use the word *linger* for synonyms or related terms unless I discuss specific differences; loafing, for such purposes, might be a lingering to avoid work; whiling away might be an oblivious, blissful idleness.

In my book *On Waiting* (2008), I thought of lingering as a temporality at once part of the experience of waiting but also outside of it; I thought of it as a form of attention, a waiting *on* rather than a waiting *for*. But the differences between these two temporalities are considerable. For one, waiting is focused on the future, lingering on the present. While every waiter waits too long, we have rarely heard a lingerer complain that she lingered too long, and if we have, involuntary lingering—in sickness or in poverty—is worse than waiting. If waiting, as I tried to show in that book, is a misunderstood and undervalued experience, it seems yet easier to think of lingering—and a book about lingering—as altogether useless and decadent. After all, we have to wait, but we usually *don't* have to linger.

Nonetheless, idleness has been a subject of philosophic interest at least since Aristotle, who valued it above industry. And while in the seventeenth and eighteenth centuries the Puritans abhorred it, the Romantics revived the idea of lingering as a condition for aesthetic and spiritual intuition. The conflict between the Puritans' moral condemnation of idleness and the Romantics' approbation of it seems largely responsible for the suspect reputation lingering has retained to this day.

One does not find lingering or its synonyms in the titles or indexes of many books, though lately there has been a resurgence of a related interest—for example Carl Honoré's *In Praise of Slowness: Challenging the Cult of Speed* (2004), or *The Slow Professor: Challenging the Culture of Speed in the Academy* by Maggie Berg and Barbara Seeber (2016), or Michelle Boulous Walker's *Slow Philosophy: Reading against the Institution* (2017). As their titles announce, these books explicitly resist a culture of speed and consumption and are written with a practical or pedagogic focus. The only book on lingering, to my knowledge, is Byung-Chul Han's Heideggerian study *The Scent of Time: A Philosophical Essay on the Art of Lingering* (2017), with which this project shares some phenomenological perspectives.

Lingering is experientially more inclusive and conceptually less definable than slowness. It is not merely the avoidance of speed or haste. It is neither a form of waiting nor a waste of time; it is neither lazy nor boring, neither useful nor useless. Lingering might be morally and pedagogically beneficial, but it can't be imposed, required, ordered, or taught. It is as resistant to external authority as it is compliant with internal motivation. It is almost impossible to account for when it occurs. For Whitman it is "a mere breath, an evanescent tinge"; and when those few "happy hours" come to him, he writes in *Specimen Days*, "(… I cannot afford to break the charm by inditing memoranda. I just abandon myself to the mood, and let it float on, carrying me in its placid ecstasy.)"[6] Evidently, such happy hours of lingering are fragile and fleeting. We recall them, as French poet Yves Bonnefoy notes, because we recall their loss. As for Whitman, though a good hundred years later, for Bonnefoy "that speck of the timeless we see glitter over and above the desert of clock-time" belongs to a world vanished in childhood and obscured "beneath the seething mass of signifiers."[7] Nonetheless, such experiences of childish idleness remain for many of us, not just for Romantic poets or hopeless daydreamers, a source of powerful poetic inspiration. "Poetry," writes Bonnefoy, "is the memory of those instants."[8]

Given the lack of definition and the conceptual indeterminacy of my subject, my references are exuberantly eclectic, including philosophical concepts by Kant, Bergson, Nietzsche, Adorno, Barthes, Benjamin, Bachelard, Blanchot, and others, and literary experiences and performances of lingering and idleness in poems by Wordsworth, Coleridge, Whitman, Rilke, Frost, and Bishop, and in novels by Woolf, Proust, and Sebald.

To the reader who has no time to read this book, I offer this brief promotional catalogue about the virtues and pleasures of lingering. Since the command "Go and linger on that old gray stone!" is patently absurd (though Wordsworth wrote a poem about it) whereas the order "Go and wait in the hall!" is perfectly commonplace, we can assume that unlike waiting, lingering is an autonomous temporality outside of and independent from the imperatives of daily life. It is supremely voluntary and therefore an experience of freedom. It is quite subversive, as our children teach us every day. There is no such thing as the beautiful without lingering. There is no poet who doesn't linger. We tell our children not to linger because we don't want them to become poets. Although it is solitary and therefore suspect, in the experience of lingering, we are freed from stifling conformities, pressures, and obligations; we discover a sense of existential and moral authenticity concealed from us in the unseemly haste of our lives. We hear the sighs of swallows swinging. We see the meadow move like water.

Many thanks to all who have supported me with their friendship and kindness during this process of writing: Greg and Irmgard Adams, Christiane Anderson, Charles Borkhuis and Kathleen Page, Kimberley and Michael Drexler, Emma Downey, Tess Gallagher, Iris and Bob Gainer, Pauline and Dave Fletcher, Denise Lewis, Pete Mackey, the late Michael Payne, Ann Tlusty and Helmut Graser, the late Charles Sackrey, Rivka Ulmer, G.C. Waldrep, Kerry Walters. To my far-flung and extended family, Paige Conn, Amaya Kirk, and Ryan Kirk; Liberty Lausterer and Micah Schweizer; Phoebe and Jeremy West and their children, my most favorite people, Heidi and Alice West, my gratitude for their love. Thank you to Waterlily, Bluegrass, and Huckleberry, who in their feline ways are experts in lingering. I am deeply grateful for my wife Saundra Kay Morris's love and support and for her unparalleled ability, not only closely to edit my writing at different stages, but also— Emerson scholar that she is—to divine what I want to say when I don't know what I want to say. Any errors or omissions in this book are of course my family's and friends' responsibilities. One writes a book in solitude, but one doesn't write it alone. May all of those dear to me linger, loaf, or while away.

Many thanks also to my wonderfully efficient editors at Routledge, Polly Dodson, Zoe Meyer, Fiona Hudson Gabuya, and Ruth Bourne.

Grateful acknowledgment to Professor Andreas Göttlich for permission to reproduce in revised form, my article "Waiting as Resistance: Lingering, Loafing, and Whiling Away" that appeared in a themed issue on waiting in *Sociologia Internationalis* (2016).

Excerpts from "The Fish" and "The Moose" from POEMS by Elizabeth Bishop. Copyright © 2011 by The Alice H. Methfessel Trust. Publisher's Note and compilation copyright © 2011 by Farrar, Straus and Giroux. Reprinted by permission of Farrar, Straus and Giroux. All Rights Reserved.

Notes

1 Walt Whitman, *Specimen Days* in *Complete Poetry and Collected Prose* (New York: Library of America, 1982), 698.
2 William Saphire, "Childhood Memories" in *Others for 1919: An Anthology of the New Verse* (New York: Nicholas L. Brown, 1920).
3 Gaston Bachelard, *The Poetics of Reverie*, trans. Daniel Russell (Boston: Beacon P, 1971), 130.
4 John Milton, *Paradise Lost*, ed. Gordon Teskey (New York: Norton, 2005), iv, 328.
5 Maurice Merleau-Ponty, *Signs*, trans. Richard C. McCleary (Chicago: Northwestern UP, 1964), 195–196.
6 Whitman, *Complete Poetry and Collected Prose*, 793.
7 Yves Bonnefoy, *The Arrière-pays*, trans. Stephen Romer (London: Seagull Books, 2012), 180–181.
8 Ibid., 191.

1 A moment, please

Emerson's moment

"Patience and patience," the American poet and philosopher Ralph Waldo Emerson exhorts at the end of his essay "Experience,"

> ...we shall win at the last. We must be very suspicious of the deceptions of the element of time. It takes a good deal of time to eat or to sleep, or to earn a hundred dollars, and very little time to entertain a hope and an insight which becomes the light of our life.[1]

It is deceptive to confuse a measurable with an immeasurable time, just as it is deceptive to think of a hundred dollars as equivalent to hope or insight. The "light of our life" cannot be purchased for a hundred dollars. "Since our office is with moments," Emerson declares earlier in the essay, "let us husband them."[2] Husbanding a moment implies the moment's cherished value and rarity; for it takes no more, but also no less, than a moment to entertain a hope and an insight.

This is a book about very little time—a little time that is a lot. Although measurably brief, Emerson's moment is paradoxically experienced as immeasurably longer than its measurement. Perhaps his moment mocks measurement altogether. We partake of such moments, I propose in this book, when we linger, to which we could add such reviled pursuits as idling, loafing, loitering, daydreaming, tarrying, dawdling, dallying, and perhaps strolling, sauntering, wandering, meandering, even sleeping (with one's eyes open)—all those languid moments and movements, all of them experienced as if in slow motion, for which our parents and teachers would have scolded us while Emerson would have praised us.

Unsurprisingly, the *Merriam Webster's Dictionary* lists as synonyms for linger: "crawl, creep, dally, dawdle, delay, diddle, dillydally, drag,

2 *A moment, please*

lag, loiter, lollygag (also lallygag), mope, poke, shilly-shally, tarry"—most of which sound naughty and wayward enough to elicit mild rebuke. Indeed, in their delightfully petulant and childishly insistent alliterations and assonances the names the *Webster's Dictionary* assigns to the experiences in question seem to derive from preverbal stages of childhood and thereafter seem hardly to have been granted more legitimacy than slothfulness. Since then, for most of us, as T.S. Eliot beautifully laments, "there is only the unattended moment," the moment "lost in a shaft of sunlight."[3]

Notwithstanding the dictionary's censorious catalog, the novelist and art historian John Berger recalls a moment of lingering in a particular field he had to cross on his way home and concludes that although "common," the experience remains mysteriously "nameless." Eliot would have agreed. Berger attempts in his brief essay nonetheless to name the experience:

> The experience which I am attempting to describe by one tentative approach after another is very precise and is immediately recognizable. But it exists at a level of perception and feeling which is probably preverbal—hence, very much, the difficulty of writing about it.[4]

This book, by one tentative approach after another, aims to examine such moments of lingering in order to discover the hope and insight, the aesthetic and ethical dimensions, harbored in such a temporality.

These same aesthetic and ethical dimensions inform an event reported in Emerson's journal entry dated April 11, 1834, about his walk to Cambridge during which he

> ... found a sunny hollow where the east wind could not blow & lay down against the side of a tree to most happy beholdings. At least I opened my eyes & let what would pass through them into the soul. I saw no more my relation how near & petty to Cambridge or Boston, I heeded no more what minute or hour our Massachusetts clocks might indicate—I saw only the noble earth on which I was born, with the great Star which warms & enlightens it.[5]

Defying the imperative of minute and hour rung from shyster Yankee clocks, Emerson's lingering announces the unmeasurable, perhaps the immeasurable, time of earth and sun. In such cosmic perspective one is temporarily freed from near and petty concerns; one's solitude enables empathy; one's eyes become portals to the soul. Emerson's entry also implies that lingering is not only an experience of time but also of place; it is an experience of the harmony of time and place.

Far from near and petty relations and oblivious of minutes and hours, Emerson's lingering in a sunny hollow is of course a Romantic commonplace; it can happen even to one who is strolling through a city, as when Emerson crosses Boston Common "in snow puddles, at twilight, under a clouded sky, without having in my thoughts any occurrence of special good fortune."[6] His poem "*Waldeinsamkeit*" (forest solitude) amounts to a manifesto on the virtues of idleness. As in the journal entry, the poet's experience, again spatially discrete, occurring in a somewhat exotically foreign-sounding location, is set in opposition to official time—"I do not count the hours" and "O what have I to do with time?"—to conclude in a celebratory stanza:

> Oblivion here thy wisdom is,
> Thy thrift, the sleep of cares;
> For a proud idleness like this
> Crowns all thy mean affairs.[7]

The stanza mentions essential features of Romanticism and lingering at once: intuition, simplicity, serenity, ethical and spiritual illumination, and in the oxymoronic "proud idleness" Emerson's conspicuous dissent from the economy of the Puritan work ethic. These oppositional features recur almost identically about one hundred years later in Robert Frost's famous poem "Stopping by Woods on a Snowy Evening" which ends, significantly, with the acknowledgment, "But I have promises to keep...."[8]

Walter Benjamin in his *Arcades Project* traces the liberating and moral effects of such temporalities to the eighteenth-century philosopher Jean-Jacques Rousseau for whom " 'solitude is a condition essential to the idler,' " and " 'the idleness of solitude is delightful because it is free and voluntary.' "[9] In a subsequent entry, Benjamin concludes that "Empathy is possible only to the solitary; solitude, therefore, is a precondition of authentic idleness."[10] Since empathy is a social trait, it may appear counterintuitive that it is in solitude that we acquire empathy, but it is only in the solitude of self-reflection that we are relatively independent from social constraints and compulsions that might force or replace authentic motivation. The promises Frost's traveler makes arise out of his solitary lingering. Hence Emerson's foregrounding of solitude in retaining the German title of his poem, *Waldeinsamkeit*.

Inauthentic idleness is not solitary; it is either coerced or merely slothful; it does not produce empathy. While the inauthentic idler simply wastes or kills time, the authentic idler does not entertain such profligate or murderous intentions. While the inauthentic idler is stuck, bored, or paralyzed, the authentic idler is transported, moved, or changed. While time for the former passes painfully slowly, time for the latter passes delightfully slowly. In short, hope, insight, and happy beholdings do not come to one who is merely lazy. If we ask ourselves what we do when we do nothing, the answer for the lazy is *nothing*—he is ostensibly impassive, perhaps even bored—whereas for the lingerer it is *something*—though she may not know what it is.

Although it is *something* that we do when we do nothing, we neither fill nor empty, neither earn nor squander our time when we linger. Neither tireless nor tired, neither vigorous nor sluggish, neither industrious nor slothful, it is hard to say what lingering is, what peculiar temporality it occupies between such oppositional terms. For Marcel Proust, whose wisdom and insights in *A la recherche du temps perdu* are based chiefly, as I will try to show, on the privilege of idleness, lingering is an effort; it requires "the mind to work upon itself"; it is clearly distinguished from laziness; it "reduce[s] to insipidity the sweets of the mental idleness that makes one prefer to abandon the effort."[11]

Lingering, then, is an internal, deeply intimate, deeply solitary state— in a solitary place, a forest perhaps, a sunny hollow, or a poem. French poet Yves Bonnefoy ponders this harmonious confluence of time and space when he observes that "the place as it exists in the mind, despite its strangeness, is in fact the same as the place in which we really are at the instant we perceive it, but it exists at a level that is more inward."[12] Although inwardness implies a hermetic, unsharable solitude, when Walt Whitman invites his reader to loaf in his poetry, he not only intimates that poetry is an inward place, but that—because it is poetry—it is a sharable inwardness. The poet's solitude is not solipsistic but social.

Rilke's *Hiersein*

For Rainer Maria Rilke authentic idleness, as he writes in the "Seventh" of his *Duino Elegies*, is a state of euphoric "*Hiersein*." Stephen Mitchell translates Rilke's term as "Truly being here,"[13] but the adverb "truly" might be redundant since "being here" is meant to be a complete realization of one's existence. For Rilke, *Hiersein* is an ecstatic, barely conscious, trancelike condition most likely experienced by animals or children—or by the dying. "There are moments in childhood," Bachelard points out, "when every child is the astonished being, the being who realizes the *astonishment of being*."[14] For us, such astonishment of being is only rarely and briefly attained, when it is, one is nothing but immeasurable duration:

> *Denn eine Stunde war jeder, vielleicht nicht*
> *ganz eine Stunde, ein mit den Massen der Zeit kaum*
> *Messliches zwischen zwei Weilen—, da sie ein Dasein*
> *hatte.*
>
> For each of you were an hour, perhaps not
> even an hour, were something hardly measurable
> by the measure of time, between two whiles—, wherein it had
> existence.[15]

Rilke's language is sufficiently thorny to cause his readers, and especially his translators, considerable trouble. Most translations assume that the girls Rilke addresses in these lines "had an hour, or a little less," *wherein* they experienced true being. Such a reading is not supported by Rilke's German. There is, for one, the pronoun *"jeder,"* meaning "each" whose masculine gender cannot refer to the girls but suggests instead a generic human being, *der Mensch* in German, which would fit the masculine. And it is not that therefore a human being is in possession of an hour of being but rather inversely that time, *die Zeit*, so to speak, takes possession of, embodies itself in, a human being. The feminine pronoun, *"sie"* in *"da sie ein Dasein / hatte,"* which I translate as "wherein *it* had / existence," refers to time, so that "it" is time that has existence in its human embodiment. In its human embodiment, the hour loses its measure; it "yields no shape" and becomes "something hardly measurable." Only birth and death put a shape and a measure to it.

I present this embodiment of time in such tedious detail only to demonstrate how easily we, and virtually all of Rilke's translators, think of time as an abstract *external* movement. But time is not passing outside of me as I write this sentence on a gloomy March day during the coronavirus pandemic. Time passes only in the duration of material phenomena. I, too, am a material phenomenon. Time is passing within me. I am the time that is passing. "Nowhere, Beloved," Rilke confirms, "will world be, but within."[16]

Rilke's thinking here not only anticipates the German philosopher Martin Heidegger's concept of authentic being in *Dasein*, but it also echoes the German late eighteenth-century philosopher Immanuel Kant's notion of internal time as an *a priori* condition of all experiences. Kant insists that time is intrinsically embodied; that synchronized clock-time,

Newtonian absolute time, is merely an abstract human construct. Kant writes in *Critique of Pure Reason* that

> Time is nothing other than the form of inner sense, i.e., of the intuition of our self and our inner state. ... And just because this inner intuition yields no shape we also attempt to remedy this lack through analogies and represent the temporal sequence through a line progressing to infinity.

And a bit further on: "Time is the *a priori* formal condition of all appearances in general."[17] Kant's notion of internal time is memorably reiterated in French philosopher Henri Bergson's phrase "it is we who are passing when we say time passes,"[18] in which, as in Kant, objective time does not exist except as an amorphous, embodied, lived duration.[19]

Kant is well aware that this inner intuition of duration cannot be named without "analogies" to a progressing, spatial line; in Bergson the linearity of the word *passing* implies just such an analogy, for we pass in succession from one place to another—in the process of which we tend to forget that it is indeed the act and quality of passing, the endurance, the velocity, the speed or slowness that determine a life, perhaps as much as or more than its external coordinates. In his book *Temporalities*, Russel West-Pavlov seems successfully to eschew this epistemological confusion between external and internal time: "Time," he explains, "is not an environment in which things happen, but it is the indefatigable happening of things which is time."[20] Here the concept of "happening" seems closely to refer to Kant's notion of the shapelessness of temporal intuition; the concept of "happening of things" and the adjective "indefatigable," moreover, refer to Kant's and Bergson's notions of the embodiment of time. Among the indefatigable happening of things, then, we are things too. Each of us is a fortuitous happening, an unrepeatable event, an unforeseeable accident. Indefatigable not in its singularity but only in its endless biological multiplicity, each of our existential happenings thus announces but a singular, existential brevity. Proust's *Swann's Way* ends poignantly with such a notion of the brief embodiment of time in material things: "... and houses, roads, avenues are as fleeting, alas, as the years."[21] In his "Ninth Elegy," Rilke similarly thinks of human lives as "the most fleeting of all."[22]

It is paradoxically within our existential and biological brevity where Bergson locates the duration that is "the continuous melody of our inner life—a melody which is going on and will go on, indivisible, from the beginning to the end of our conscious existence. Our personality is precisely that." Although he thinks of this melody as "the very stuff of our existence," we are so enamored, Bergson deplores, with external, spatial representations of time that "we have no interest in listening to the uninterrupted humming of life's depth."[23] Indeed, so true is Bergson's pronouncement that we find it daily confirmed in our lives where we prefer the analogy of "a line" (to repeat Kant's point) to the experience of time as "inner sense"; we are, in other words, not interested in how time passes but merely in its measurable markers and components and, as we shall see, its reifications. Thus, we tend not to appreciate a stone, a flower, a poem, or a melody as a temporality, but merely as a composition of minerals, cells, signs, or sounds. To redirect this focus from an object's components to its ontology would be to ask—admittedly somewhat oddly—how does this stone, this painting, this butterfly endure? How does this fugue pass from voice to voice? How slow is this Grecian urn? How gently does the light fall in Bernardo Bellotto's luminous landscapes?

There are several instances in Proust's novel where Bergson's melody of our inner life is replayed. In one of these examples of Bergson's influence, Proust suggests that listening to the uninterrupted humming of life's depth may confront us with unexamined, perhaps unsettling existential realizations: for "the field open to the musician," he writes, "is not a miserable scale of seven notes, but an immeasurable keyboard still almost entirely unknown" that awakens "that great unpenetrated and disheartening darkness of our soul which we take for emptiness and nothingness."[24] Proust's "immeasurable keyboard" not only implies the Kantian notion of the shapelessness of our intuition of time, but his phrase also offers a felicitous metaphor for the difference between the bad and the good musician. The bad musician waits; the good musician lingers. While waiting, as we know, usually plays itself out on a miserable scale of seven notes, experiences of lingering are composed on an immeasurable keyboard; they connect us to those deeper, internal human dimensions, the humming of life's depth, the melody of duration, the darkness of our soul. Proust's suggestion that we may take—or mistake—the darkness of the soul merely for emptiness and nothingness leaves open the possibility—to be explored in these pages—that these deeper temporal dimensions may harbor more auspicious, happier insights, such as are implied in Rilke's ecstatic experience of *Hiersein*.

Unlike waiting, lingering has porous temporal borders; it occurs immeasurably between whiles. We recognize the openness of these temporal borders in the animal's face, as Rilke beautifully proposes in the "Eighth" of his *Duino Elegies*. For Rilke, the animal looks not *at* but *through* death: "when it moves, it moves / in eternity." We, by contrast, never have "before us that pure space into which the flowers / open endlessly."[25] Evidently, animals linger. Perhaps we could learn it from them. In the temporality of lingering, as Whitman proclaims, "there is really no death."[26] For Bachelard, "In a reverie, the word 'death' is vulgar."[27]

Timeless stillness

In one of Henry David Thoreau's allegories, "Time is but the stream I go a-fishing in. I drink at it; but while I drink, I see the sandy bottom and detect how shallow it is. Its thin current slides away, but eternity remains."[28] Thoreau's conceit echoes what Kant calls the analogy that we imagine because the intuition of time "yields no shape." While time is indeed shallow and flows alarmingly away, it is not the space of the sandy bottom that opens time to eternity; it is the temporality of "while I drink." One might fall into this eternity of "while." One might never drink enough of it. One might endlessly revisit it. Nor is it the linear temporality of the stream that constitutes "our self and our inner state," but the quiet whiling away in this inner state.

For Bachelard—a Romantic like Whitman or Thoreau—the eternity that remains is "the great calm lake where time rests from its flowing. And this lake is within us, like a primitive water, like the environment in which an immobile childhood continues to reside."[29] In such aqueous contexts one finds oneself quite worried about Rilke's wayward child in his "Eighth Elegy" who "may wander there for hours, through the timeless / stillness, may get lost in it ...."[30] It is such waters, lakes, and moments of timeless stillness—all of them metaphors for the enchantingly mellow and liquid slowness of lingering—that are the subject of this book. "[W]hen the passage of time is broken," Bonnefoy writes, "a fragrance of eternity is sometimes released."[31] Bonnefoy's metaphor intimates the temporal extension, intensification, or prolongation that we experience when time seems to stand still. But of course it only *seems* to stand still. Although its passage may seem broken, although it may seem like a great calm lake where time rests from its flowing, time is never still. It is in each instant embodied and therefore moving; in each instant it composes our self and our inner state. While the waiter's impatience embodies the accelerated speed of this movement, the lingerer's tranquility manifests its slowness—a slowness that approximates stillness, a stillness that we experience like an eternity.

The poetic imagination, as the following examples show, is rooted in the auditory, visual, atmospheric, and bodily dimensions of such ecstatic slowness. Early on in "Song of Myself" Whitman proclaims, "I lean and loafe at my ease observing a spear of summer grass,"[32] which initiates the languid pace of the poem. In Wordsworth's sonnet "It Is a Beauteous Evening," "The holy time is quiet as a Nun"—quietness being an essential quality of holiness.[33] Virginia Woolf's novel *Mrs. Dalloway* opens with "a particular hush, or solemnity; an indescribable pause; a suspense"[34] that announces the novel's principal, lyric temporality wherein Mrs. Dalloway performs her "idiosynchratic mnemonic time-roaming" as West-Pavlov very finely puts it.[35] "I had to run to rejoin my father and grandfather, who were calling me surprised that I had not followed them," writes Proust in *Swann's Way*. For of course, Marcel has fallen behind again and lingers: "I found it all humming with the smell of hawthorns."[36] All of W.G. Sebald's novels, in the meandering slowness of their style, resist what I call the weight of time. In one of his novels, Sebald wonders, "How strange it is, to be standing leaning against the current of time,"[37] while in another we hear of an epiphanic, lyrical moment outside of time "so peaceful it was as if nothing evil had ever happened anywhere on earth."[38] In a poem by Ada Limón we read, "I sat alone in the car by the post office and just *was* / for a whole hour, no one knowing how to find me...."[39] Absent from the world, here the speaker is nothing but the hour that passes. Berger concludes the essay from which I quoted above: "Suddenly an experience of disinterested observation opens ... and gives birth to a happiness which is instantly recognisable as your own."[40]

Untimeliness

Who has not as a child dillydallied in bed or in the sandpile when one should have eaten one's breakfast or cleaned one's room? Who has not found herself fallen behind, leaning against the current of time, lost in thought miles away from obligations? Who has not lingered in the driveway before entering the house, or in the parking lot before going to the post office? We linger every day. But in spite of their daily occurrence, these experiences remain nameless to the extent that they remain solitary, private, secret, unsanctioned, untimely—even a tad illicit, like stopping by woods on snowy evenings. No wonder the traveler in that poem, looking over his shoulder, must reassure himself, "He will not see me stopping here...."[41]

In his book *The Arrière Pays*, Bonnefoy thinks of such enchanting experiences of untimeliness as simultaneously near and far, present and absent:

> The world which was, yesterday, so intimately lived, and somehow understood, has from now on become, in a deep way, enigmatic.

> The little garden where we used to play, with its tree, has now become both intensely close and mysteriously silent. A bird sings, we do not know from where, and we are astonished, it is both present and absent. Someone passes by on the road, halts for a moment in the light of evening, and there is the same moment of epiphany but this time hidden in a mystery—for the unity encountered so closely yesterday in everything has now withdrawn underneath an appearance which is visible, but as though seen against the light, an object as much of anxiety as of nostalgic yearning.[42]

What is remarkable, for our purposes, in each of these paradisical archetypes—the garden, the tree, the bird, the twilight encounter—is that each seems itself lingering in time, each immobilized by a ceasing or stopping—a silence, a veiling, a halting—and thus symbolic of a rest or repose that seems no longer attainable to the speaker. Ironically, it is in the very "appearance" of these phenomena, or when they reappear in "a discourse set on reifying all things,"[43] that these reveries are "withdrawn" and resurface only as anxiety and nostalgia. Anxiety and nostalgia form the warp and weft of the lingerer's loom; when she is anxious, her thread of time tears; when she is nostalgic, her thread of time tangles.

Perhaps my reader (meanwhile) hopes no one will see her stopping in this book, or perhaps she will manage to abscond from her obligations in these pages and has to be shaken back like Rilke's child. For experiences of lingering offer hope and insight that the times wherein we eat, sleep, and make a hundred dollars never allow. Even that most inconsolable of melancholics, E.M. Cioran, concedes that "The idle apprehend more things, are deeper than the industrious...."[44]

Duration, not time

The untimely temporality of lingering that I explore in this book resonates in a variety of philosophic terms and traditions besides the ones—chiefly in Kant and Bergson—I've already mentioned: Aristotle's episodic as opposed to sequential unfolding of plot; Hegel's lyric versus spatial structure of the epic; Bachelard's poetic verticality versus prosaic horizontality; Husserl's internal time-consciousness as opposed to objective time; Heidegger's authentic versus inauthentic existence;[45] Kristeva's contrast between the embodied semiotic and the abstract symbolic; Deleuze and Guattari's subversive rhizomatic versus the canonical arboreal structure; "modernism's resistance to 'the one, true time' of the public clock";[46] and a host of literary texts: Penelope's daily weaving and nightly unweaving; Hamlet's episodic deviations from the predictable revenge tragedy he should enact; Baudelaire's *idéal*, realm of remembrance versus the torment of time in the *spleen*; Proust's *mémoire involontaire* and *mémoire volontaire*; Faulkner's "juxtaposition of racialized lag with industrial progress"[47]; the "untimely ... nonsequential, asynchronous experiences of time" examined in queer and race studies.[48] Much work has been done, evidently, on these opposing temporalities wherein a subjective temporality is measured, positively or negatively, against an officially sanctioned linear temporality.

Notes

1 *Emerson's Prose and Poetry*, ed. Joel Porte and Saundra Morris (New York: Norton, 2001), 212.
2 Ibid., 204.
3 T.S. Eliot, *Four Quartets* in *The Complete Poems and Plays* (London: Faber and Faber, 1985), 190.
4 John Berger, *About Looking* (New York: Vintage, 1980), 200.
5 *Emerson's Prose and Poetry*, 493.
6 Ibid., 29.
7 Ibid., 477–478.
8 Robert Frost, *Collected Poems, Prose, and Plays* (New York: Library of America, 1970), 207.
9 Walter Benjamin, *The Arcades Project*, trans. Howard Eiland and Kevin McLaughlin (The Belknap P of Harvard UP, 2003), 805.
10 Ibid.
11 Marcel Proust, *In the Shadow of Young Girls in Flower*, trans. James Grieve (New York: Penguin Books, 2005), 297.
12 Bonnefoy, *The Arrière-pays*, 168.
13 *The Selected Poetry of Rainer Maria Rilke*, trans. Stephen Mitchell (New York: Vintage, 1989), 189.
14 Bachelard, *The Poetics of Reverie*, 116.
15 Rainer Maria Rilke, *Die Gedichte* (Frankfurt am Main: Insel, 1987), 655; my trans.
16 Ibid.
17 Immanuel Kant, *Critique of Pure Reason*, trans. Paul Guyer and Allen W. Wood (Cambridge: Cambridge UP, 1998), B 50, 163; see also A 31, 162: "Time is a necessary representation that grounds all intuitions. In regard to appearances in general one cannot remove time, though one can very well take the appearances away from time. Time is therefore given *a priori*. In it alone is all actuality of appearances possible. The latter could all disappear, but time itself, as the universal condition of their possibility, cannot be removed."
18 Henri Bergson, *Duration and Simultaneity* in *Bergson: Key Writings*, ed. Keith Ansell Pearson and John Mullarkey (New York: Continuum, 2002), 216.
19 Merleau-Ponty echoes these Kantian and Bergsonian notions of internal time when he writes, "...it [time] is nothing that I see from without. From without, I would only have the trail of time; I would not be present at its

generative thrust. So, time is myself; I am the duration that I grasp, and time is duration grasped in me" (*Signs*, 184).
20 Russell West-Pavlov, *Temporalities* (London: Routledge, 2012), 84. The German word *Augenblick*, West-Pavlov argues earlier in the book, understood as a Heideggerian "epiphanic instant of decision," also seeks to avoid this pitfall (45).
21 Marcel Proust, *Swann's Way*, trans. Lydia Davis (New York: Penguin Books, 2003), 444.
22 Rilke, *Die Gedichte*, 661.
23 Henri Bergson, *The Creative Mind* in *Key Writings*, 260, 216, 261; cf. Hegel's very similar claim that "musical time" is "a real reflection of our spiritual nature, or rather that of the fundamental truth of self-identity," G.W.F. Hegel, *The Philosophy of Fine Art*, trans. F.B. Osmaston (New York: Hacker Art, 1975), 333–334; cf. also Husserl in West-Pavlov, 43. It is likely Bergson's philosophy that informs Rilke's ecstatic *Hiersein*.
24 Proust, *Swann's Way*, 362–363.
25 Rilke, *Die Gedichte*, 658; my trans.
26 Whitman, *Complete Poetry and Collected Prose*, 194.
27 Bachelard, *The Poetics of Reverie*, 111.
28 Henry D. Thoreau, *Walden, Civil Disobedience and Other Writings* (New York: Norton, 2008), 70.
29 Bachelard, *The Poetics of Reverie*, 111.
30 *Rilke,* trans. Mitchell, 193.
31 Bonnefoy, *The Arrière-pays*, 62.
32 Whitman, *Complete Poetry and Collected Prose*, 27.
33 William Wordsworth, *William Wordsworth* (Oxford: Oxford UP, 1988), 281.
34 Virginia Woolf, *Mrs. Dalloway* (New York: Harcourt Brace & Co., 1981), 4.
35 West-Pavlov, *Temporalities*, 20.
36 Proust, *Swann's Way*, 140.
37 W.G. Sebald, *Vertigo*, trans. Michael Hulse (New York: New Directions, 1999), 46.
38 W.G. Sebald, *The Emigrants*, trans. Michael Hulse (New York: New Directions, 1996), 217.
39 Ada Limón, *The Carrying: Poems* (Minneapolis: Milkweed Editions, 2018), 13.
40 Berger, *About Looking*, 204–205.
41 Frost, *Collected Poems, Prose, and Plays*, 207.
42 Bonnefoy, *The Arrière Pays*, 179.
43 Ibid., 182.
44 E.M. Cioran, *A Short History of Decay*, trans. Richard Howard (New York: Arcade Publishing, 1998), 23.
45 For a concise discussion of Heidegger's philosophy of time, see Byung-Chul Han, *The Scent of Time: A Philosophical Essay on the Art of Lingering* (London: Polity P, 2017), esp. chapter 9.
46 Charles M. Tung, "Technology and Time: Clocks, Time Machines, and Speculation" in Thomas M. Allen, ed. *Time and Literature* (Cambridge: Cambridge UP, 2018), 169.
47 Ibid., 176.
48 Jeffrey Insko, "Historicism" in Allen, 184.

2 The temporality of the beautiful

The beautiful and the good

We wait in measurable time; we linger in duration. While "the time of towns is tolled from the world by funereal chimes,"[1] as Emerson deplores, the time of lingering is neither rung from authoritative clocks nor is it funereal. It is subjective, solitary, private, internal, indivisible, transient but endless, felt rather than known, lived rather than measured. In Kant's philosophy, internal duration, as we have said, is defined as a temporality that constitutes the subject.[2] In Kant's *aesthetic* theory, the human and the aesthetic dimensions of this temporality overlap; there, Kant defines the aesthetic not as an object but as a fleetingly subjective event: a consciousness, an experience, a feeling, a happening, a free play of the imagination, a free lawfulness.[3] All of these terms correlate with Bergson's concept of duration, and all of them are conditioned—nowadays inconceivably—by the absence of interest or desire.[4] Bergson's *durée*, like Kant's beautiful, is existential; it constitutes who we are; it is the melody of our inner life. Lingering (to appropriate Benjamin's reflections on Baudelaire) "is—if one follows Bergson—the actualization of the *durée* which rids man's soul of obsession with time."[5] It happens "suddenly," as Berger notes, "instantly," and without interest. One doesn't know, as those who lose themselves in lingering or daydreaming often confess, how one got there.

If Kant did not propose that in the experience of the beautiful interest must be suspended, we would conclude that the beautiful is something to be desired and therefore to be (impatiently) waited for. It could perhaps be purchased for a hundred dollars, ordered on-line, put on a syllabus, or acquired for the price of admission to the museum. If, on the other hand, desire is suspended in the experience of the beautiful, then we merely linger in its presence—and perchance it might play its melody in us. The aesthetic, in other words, is a temporal, embodied experience; it is free and voluntary. It is not institutional. It is, perhaps surprisingly, ethical.

The idea of the ethical dimension of the aesthetic occurs to Kant almost as an afterthought, late in the *Critique of Judgment* when, perilously endangering his claim that the beautiful is a purposive purposelessness, he declares abruptly and no sooner than in the penultimate 59th chapter "*das Schöne ist das Symbol des Sittlichguten*"[6] (the beautiful is the symbol of morality). But Kant's conclusion is not surprising. The beautiful is not only from the very beginning of the *Critique of Judgment*, as Jonathan Loesberg points out, "a symbolic embodiment of a moral view of nature,"[7] but the beautiful is the symbol of morality because both the aesthetic and the ethical relation ought to presuppose a suspension of (self) interest. Kant's notions of disinterestedness or indifference in the aesthetic experience are embodied in a mental lingering often accompanied by its physical enactment, for example in the secluded "sunny hollow" sought out by Emerson.

The most illuminating explanation, to my knowledge, of the conjunction of the aesthetic with the ethical is offered by poet and philosopher Susan Stewart, who proposes in *The Open Studio: Essays on Art and Aesthetics* an "ethics as practiced or modeled in aesthetic experience." Based on the "structural analogy" between Kant's aesthetic and Emmanuel Levinas' ethics, Stewart suggests that "Kant's *Critique of Judgment* offers a paradigm for aesthetic experience as an encounter between persons and forms that is in truth an encounter between persons"; it is above all, she goes on, a non-teleological encounter whose ethical dimension resides in its disinterestedness, "a form of vigilant passivity toward the face of the other."[8] In her more recent *The Poet's Freedom: A Notebook on Making*, Stewart echoes these philosophic affinities by insisting that "a poetic mood ... is not simply to be passive but also ... receptive, alert to something in the circumstances of the present without quite knowing what will happen next."[9]

It is such a form of vigilant passivity, or passive receptivity, that I associate in these pages with the embodied aesthetic experience of lingering. In her book *Slow Philosophy*, Michelle Boulous Walker attributes a similar oxymoron as that between passivity and vigilance to the experience of wonder encountered in contemplative meditation: "Wonder involves rest and contemplation, a kind of temporary withdrawal that is simultaneously active and passive."[10] This dual aspect of lingering, its passive activity, its passionate indifference, its languid ecstasy, is also implied in Whitman's "I lean and loafe at my ease observing..." or in Sebald's "leaning against the current of time," for leaning is already inclination and curiosity but also repose and relaxation. Kant's concept of aesthetic indifference, in sum, is the mental equivalent of the experience of lingering. Lingering embodies and performs aesthetic indifference. Just as the person who prays assumes a bodily position in accord with her spiritual endeavors, the bodily position of the person who lingers inclines her, leans her, towards the perception of the beautiful.

Since I have suggested, with reference to Rousseau and the Romantics, that idleness is solitary, I want to emphasize that such solitude is a prerequisite for empathy in so far as an ethical judgment has to be attained through a *solitary* inner conviction, not by social pressure. And since I claim, perhaps somewhat oddly, that lingering is a qualified *activity* not merely a lazy passivity, I want to qualify that in its suspension of interest lingering is indeed passive—embodied in the lingerer's posture—but in its vigilance it is active—embodied in the lingerer's attention enabled by his passivity. These complementary qualities are exemplified as much in Freud's patient reclining on the psychoanalytical couch as in Emerson's reclining position "against the side of a tree" that results—one hopes for Freud's patient as well—in the opening of his eyes to "let what would pass through them into the soul." Emerson's stopping, his finding of a sunny hollow where the east wind could not blow, and his considering of the noble earth and the great Star are, despite appearances, physical and mental activities that engender (his) life and work. It is a fine-tuned, solitary, solemn activity, such a lingering; for while it demands of us the relinquishing of near and petty relations, it also calls for a mental opening towards larger perspectives; while it demands a forsaking of minutes and hours, it also calls us to live in a temporality ordered by natural and cosmic rhythms.

In his article "Lingering, Pleasure, Desire, and Life in Kant's *Critique of Judgment*," Robert Lehman excellently defines the dialectical, complementary temporality of this active passivity in Kant's aesthetic as a movement. "There is movement in this contemplation, certainly," he writes, "which Kant describes transcendentally as free-play and empirically as lingering, enjoying, doing something by doing nothing."[11] Here the movement of contemplation, free-play, and lingering entails a similarly nuanced dialectic as that between vigilance and passivity.

But what is the *something* that Lehman mentions that one does by doing *nothing*? Lingering, to be sure, may seem merely contemplative, unproductive, useless, passive, but in its embodied calm it harbors a quiet, subversive vigilance. The child's dawdling in his room while he is called for supper, the adult's daydreaming in the car while the clock ticks, the student's lingering in Whitman's "Song of Myself" while the professor waits, all these moments of quiet rebellion against the dictates of official time call us forth into intimate encounters; they foster inclinations for the experience of the beautiful, they are, as Proust will show, vocational. Lingering, then, is a mental precondition for the writing of books in search of lost time, for example. When Whitman invites his reader, "Stop this day and night with me and you shall possess the origin of all poems,"[12] it is neither the day nor the night but the stopping that promises such transgressive revelations. The *something* that one does while doing *nothing* is not a thing but an activity—though most often this activity remains secret and invisible to an observer, nor does this activity often result in a hefty novel like Proust's or an abundant poem like Whitman's.

We wish our children were allowed to linger in Rilke's timeless stillness. We wish our students would stop in Whitman's poem to become good loafers on God's handkerchief. But one can't be told to linger.

Play

One can't wait for the beautiful. But one can linger in it. The beautiful happens—but only to one who lingers; it is not a thing but something that *happens*—a word repeated by Kant in his aesthetic philosophy. "[W]hat is in play here," Jean-François Lyotard explains, "is not the 'recognition' of the given, as Kant says, but the ability to let things come as they present themselves." And a little further on: "Aesthetic pleasure 'befalls' the mind like grace, an 'inspiration.' "[13] "Artworks," as Theodor Adorno claims, "are only completely perceptible in *temps durée*, the conception of which Bergson probably derived from artistic experience."[14] Stewart suggests that works of art offer "an alternative to the grid of temporality driven by instrumental reason."[15] "Once the culture of rest or *otium* vanishes," she argues in *The Poet's Freedom*, "it is not easy to fall into a mood or a daydream. To play, to create free, even random comparisons, to risk error and 'give it a try,' all require independence from both the true urgencies of hunger and shelter and the imaginary urgencies of entertainment."[16] Stewart's distinction between true and imaginary urgencies—the latter echoing Marx's notion of manufactured desire—is poignantly relevant in our time, when the two motivations are easily confused. For play is not just entertainment. The German Romantic poet and playwright Friedrich Schiller points out that children play *mit heiligem Ernst*, with holy earnestness. Play is a serious matter.

Precisely because she plays while her paternal companion composes the "solemn thought" of his poem, the girl in Wordsworth's sonnet "It Is a Beauteous Evening" has her being in the temporality of the beautiful. While for Wordsworth the beautiful is a manifestation of divinity, for the girl this divinity is her very "nature"; it is hence unconscious;

her nature, in other words, is the gratuitousness of divinity's incarnation. She lies "in Abraham's bosom all the year." As she embodies time, she embodies divinity, "God being with thee when we know it not." It is in our not-knowing that such divinity manifests itself. Both the form of the sonnet and its descriptive exaltation of nature suggest that such not-knowing of the divine comes about in and through the temporality of the beautiful. All one has to do, Wordsworth seems to suggest, is look and listen. Though "it is not easy," to recall Stewart's phrase, "to fall into a mood or a daydream."

Embodiment

In his book on the poetry of Wallace Stevens, Simon Critchley thinks of poetry as "an experience of the world as meditation, the mind slowing in front of things, the mind pushing back against the pressure of reality through the minimal transfigurations of the imagination."[17] While Critchley's argument befits Stevens' antagonisms between imagination and reality, Wordsworth's example implies a less antagonistic theory of slowness. Here aesthetic experience is determined not by "the mind pushing back" but by the mind opening to let things come, to what befalls the mind like grace.

An aesthetic of lingering, we have said, is *embodied*. Although the beautiful is experienced by the suspension of interest and desire in Kant's aesthetic, it is there nonetheless most fundamentally embodied. The absence of interest and desire leaves in the encounter with the beautiful nothing but the naked human presence. Kant's aesthetic, to say this more simply, is the only aesthetic theory whose sole prerequisite is that I show up. It is the least demanding, most democratic of all theories, hence his claim—much misunderstood and thus maligned—that the subjective experience of the beautiful is universal. The thrift and simplicity of this aesthetic requirement is exemplified by Emerson in lying down against the side of a tree, by Whitman in leaning and loafing, by Wordsworth in sitting on an old gray stone, by Coleridge in resting under a lime-tree bower, by Frost in stopping by snowy woods or in the swinging of birches. The point is: one doesn't need an appointment, a ticket, or a diploma for it. One needs to be present. One needs merely to lie in Abraham's bosom. Such presence cannot be purchased, taught, or required. It is the most fundamental requirement in Levinas for the ethical acknowledgment of the other, the expression of which is a gratuitous, "here I am."[18]

The *human*, in these embodied moments, is a temporality implied in the Greek term *aion*. "When Heraclitus tells us that *aion* is a child playing, he thereby depicts as play the temporalizing essence of the living being," as we read in Giorgio Agamben's "Reflections on History and Play."[19] Only when one plays, Schiller says to the same effect, is one truly human.[20] Crucial to Agamben's argument is that this play constitutes the child's "historicity."[21] History, in this radical sense, is not the temporal realm where one makes a hundred dollars. History is not *chronos*, one damn thing after another; "history," Agamben writes in a different essay (and this is also implied in Kant and Schiller), "is not...man's servitude to continuous linear time, but man's liberation from it."[22] Art as a version of play, in this sense, is an activity wherein the omnipotence of time, of death, and of money is suspended.

Poignantly, when French philosopher Maurice Blanchot observes that "He who dies cannot tarry,"[23] he who dies eminently loses his ability to liberate himself from history; he is, as we flippantly say, history. To linger, to tarry, to saunter, to loaf, to stand still, to stop, to play—these are ways of liberation; these are aesthetic temporalities; these are ways of resistance against the hegemony of death that is money time. This is a book in praise of wasting time.

Notes

1 "The Poet" in *Emerson's Prose and Poetry*, 197.
2 Cf. Paul Ricoeur, *Memory, History, Forgetting*, trans. Kathleen Blamey and David Pellauer (Chicago: U of Chicago P, 2004), 97.
3 The conjunction of temporality and the reflective aesthetic experience is already implied in Kant's earlier distinction between external spatial and internal temporal perception where both space and time are "relations ... that attach to the form of intuition" (Kant, *Critique of Pure Reason*, B 38, 157).
4 See for example, Barbara Herrnstein Smith's influential book, *Contingencies of Value: Alternative Perspectives for Critical Theory* (Cambridge, Mass.: Harvard UP, 1988); or Rachel Zuckert, *Kant on Beauty and Biology* (Cambridge: Cambridge UP, 2003).
5 Walter Benjamin, *Illuminations*, trans. Harry Zohn (New York: Schocken Books, 1968), 180.
6 Immanuel Kant, *Kritik der Urteilskraft* (Hamburg: Verlag von Felix Meiner, 1974), 213; Kant also considers the development of the moral inclination through the aesthetic experience in § 42.
7 Jonathan Loesberg, *A Return to Aesthetics* (Stanford: Stanford UP, 2005), 142; see also 53–56.
8 Susan Stewart, *The Open Studio: Essays on Art and Aesthetics* (Chicago: U of Chicago P., 2005), 21, 19, 20.
9 Susan Stewart, *The Poet's Freedom: A Notebook on Making* (Chicago: U of Chicago P, 2011), 57–58.
10 Michelle Boulous Walker, *Slow Philosophy: Reading against the Institution* (London: Bloomsbury, 2018), 96.

11 Robert Lehman, "Lingering, Pleasure, Desire, and Life in Kant's *Critique of Judgment*," *The Journal of Speculative Philosophy* 32, 2 (2018): 234.
12 Whitman, *Complete Poetry and Collected Prose*, 189.
13 Jean-François Lyotard, *The Inhuman: Reflections on Time*, trans. Geoffrey Bennington and Rachel Bowlby (Stanford: Stanford UP, 1991), 32, 33.
14 Theodor Adorno, *Aesthetic Theory*, trans. Robert Hullot-Kentor (Minneapolis: U of Minnesota P, 1997), 69.
15 Susan Stewart, *Poetry and the Fate of the Senses*, (Chicago: U of Chicago P, 2002), 224.
16 Stewart, *The Poet's Freedom*, 201.
17 Simon Critchley, *Things Merely Are: Philosophy in the Poetry of Wallace Stevens* (London: Routledge, 2005), 88.
18 Emmanuel Levinas, *Entre Nous: Thinking-of-the Other*, trans. Michael B. Smith and Barbara Harshav (New York: Columbia UP, 1998), 149, 169.
19 Giorgio Agamben, *Infancy and History: The Destruction of Experience*, trans. Liz Heron (London: Verso, 2007), 82.
20 Friedrich Schiller, *Über die Ästhetische Erziehung des Menschen* in *Philosophische und Gemischte Schriften* (Basel: Birkhäuser Verlag, 1968), 139.
21 Agamben, *Infancy and History*, 82.
22 Ibid., 115.
23 Maurice Blanchot, *The Space of Literature*, trans. Ann Smock (Lincoln: U of Nebraska P, 1982), 257.

3 The economics of waiting

The waiter's things

The very fluidity by which the maxim *time-is-money* rolls off the tongue, the definitional copulative, the authoritative compactness of the phrase forbidding any dispute, instantly censors the thought that time might have any other than exchange value. It is a time that perforce must be spent, translated, converted into something other than itself. The metaphor, as metaphor, performs this translation, its formal compactness epitomizing the haste and alacrity by which this conversion is to happen. The resolute foregrounding of its economics is to render time itself inconspicuous; time is to appear and to exist only in its disguises: the wares, the trinkets, the diversions, the necessities exchanged for it. Time, like money, as John Berger notes, "has no content," but it can be "exchanged for the content it lacks."[1]

Waiting is an economics. The waiter[2] wants, falls short, has not, lacks; the less someone has to wait, the more she has. Waiting is a marker of inferior economic and social status, which is why Vladimir and Estragon in Samuel Beckett's *Waiting for Godot* are tramps not CEOs of pharmaceutical companies. Social and economic strata, as we well know, are determined, enforced, and ritually performed by and within strategic impositions of waiting. For a good many of us, especially those of us living with little or no social or economic advantage, not much has changed in the more than hundred years since Kafka's parable of the man who waits in vain to gain entrance to the Law. And not much, those same would add, has changed in the more than fifty or so years since Martin Luther King, Jr. lamented, "one hundred years [have] passed since emancipation, with no profound effect on [black people's] plight."[3] Today as then, the imposition of waiting is used as an instrument of class, race, rank, and gender distinctions and discrimination; it is attributed, applied, apportioned to solidify hierarchies and prejudices, and, most fundamentally, to signal an individual's or a group's existential expendability. When their waiting, despite its strategic and administered prolongations, comes to an end, when the door opens or the line shortens, it is as if the waiter were given a little of her life back by receiving permission to return, for a time, into the purgatory of those who "get things done," as Nietzsche deplores, with "unseemly and immoderate hurry-skurry."[4] But Kafka's lowly *Mann vom Lande*, who will die waiting rather than gain entrance to the Law, exemplifies, as King also put it, that waiting, for the socially and politically marginalized, "has almost always meant Never."[5]

Ironically, our very strategies of resistance against such social and political determinations are also complicit with them. Since nobody likes to wait, we strenuously try to repress, mask, or deny our waiting by distractions that are as bad as, or worse than, the waiting itself: the musac while we are put on hold on the phone; the news or sports channel in the hotel lobby; the magazines on ice-curling, fly fishing, or prostate surgery in the waiting room; the cigarettes; the chips; the chewing gum. If there is a political dimension to these distractions, then it might be precisely that they are to distract us from the realization that we are waiting.

What is so exasperating, then, about the experience of waiting, is that in waiting time itself is annoyingly conspicuous. This is essentially what constitutes what in *On Waiting* I have called the scandal of *Waiting for Godot*, where nothing but time itself is shockingly on display.[6] "Time is usually transparent," Lars Svendsen observes in *A Philosophy of Boredom*, "and it does not appear as a something. But in our confrontation with a nothing in boredom, where time is not filled with anything that can occupy our attention, we experience time as time."[7] Or worse, rather than experiencing time as time, in boredom I experience time as *myself*. I am time, therefore I am. I am nothing but time, and I feel it drain away. Since "we have no interest in listening to the uninterrupted humming of life's depth," as Bergson reminds us, since "it is we who are passing when we say time passes," the gratuitousness of the waiter's time amounts to a sense of his existential accident and redundancy. I am passing. I'm passing away. The waiter is thus subject to existential inflation—he has too much time—and devaluation—his time is worthless, nobody wants it. Nobody wants him. He restlessly seeks to escape his waiting, to grasp any bargain to stem the steady drain and dribbling away of the time that is his life. He gets up, he paces, he sits down, he looks at his phone, he surfs the web, he grabs a magazine from the rack, all with the characteristically divided attention of the waiter who is always on the lookout for a better deal and into the avidity of whose gaze anything—the dust on that lampshade, the headline in the paper, the *Sandals* vacation ad on TV—comes with the promise of escape from the waiter's unworthy existence. The reason why the waiter feels as if he is stalked by lampshades or magazines involves a certain "property," as Bergson explains, "that things outside us have," and whose uncanny quality is that "without themselves enduring," things "manifest[] themselves in our duration."[8] They have taken possession of us. I am as old as a newspaper; I am as boring as a lampshade.

The very thing that is to kill the waiter's time kills the waiter herself—at least briefly and in installments. I hold in my coffee cup the urn of my own ashes. I read in my tablet my own obituary. I glimpse in the spot of dirt under my fingernail my own insignificance. And yet, to allow oneself a brief death in the cathartic substitution of a thing for the endlessly ragged incompletions of time, to allow oneself to be etherized like a patient on a table, that is the purpose of *People* magazine, the computer game, the lightly salted pretzel. The banal, fragile, obsolescent triviality of the things the entertainment industry supplies liberates the waiter from the intimacy of his own narcissistic self-absorption and functions as a metonymy for the forgettable incident of his own existence—the waiter who has measured out his life in coffee spoons.

Prufrock's coffee spoons

The waiter's vexed negotiations between time and things are borne out in T. S. Eliot's famous poem "The Love Song of J. Alfred Prufrock," from where I borrowed the coffee spoons and where the word "time" and its predicative and conjunctive performances are compulsively repeated throughout. Time "[b]efore the taking of a toast and tea" and time "after tea and cakes and ices"[9] ever stretches void and vast before and after Prufrock like the desert of time in Marvell's "To His Coy Mistress" that Eliot echoes. But unlike Marvell who lustily complains that "at my back I always hear / Time's wingèd chariot hurrying near,"[10] Prufrock lacks amorous initiative or strategy. Unlike Marvell, who would like to linger on his mistress's various body parts if he had world enough and time—

> A hundred years should go to praise
> Thine eyes, and on thy forehead gaze.
> Two hundred to adore each breast:
> But thirty thousand to the rest.
> An age at least to every part,
> And the last age should show your heart

—Prufrock, altogether devoid of Marvell's cunning hyperboles, timidly ogles "[a]rms that lie along a table." It is only when he observes, with sudden, shocking intimacy, that "(in the lamplight [they are] downed with light brown hair!)," that the human, sexual aspect of the arm—bashfully understated and at the same time shyly foregrounded by the parentheses and by the startlingly tender word "downed"—suddenly transports him into the temporality of lingering.[11] Here, then, Prufrock, whose frustrated desire otherwise defines him as a waiter, briefly and as if in parentheses, becomes the lingerer he cannot be.

Invariably, even such unexpected, brief transformations cannot prevent the waiter's ennui about the repeatability and exchangeability of all things: "And I have known the arms already, known them all— / Arms that are braceleted and white and bare"—and we know that nothing, no teacup, cake, ice, or arm can deliver him from time. What comes "[a]fter the novels, after the teacups, after the skirts that trail along the floor," as Prufrock realizes with growing alarm, is merely more time.

Prufrock's excess of time and its monotonous replays are ritualistically performed by fashionable women in trailing skirts and shawls over their arms balancing saucers and teacups: "In the room the women come and go / Talking of Michelangelo," which scant two lines, although only repeated once, seem yet oppressively to pervade the entire poem. The couplet's ditzy double rhyme in the repetition of the two syllables, "... and go /...ange-lo" intones the suffocating pressures of social assimilation. The article "the" implies the room's and the women's specificity and anonymity at once. Unlike the lingerer whose place harmonizes with, or even embodies, his time, the waiter's space is uncanny, both familiar and strange. If Prufrock envies the ease of the women's drawing-room ballet with the great, sensuous master as they move in their excessively posed and studied ways, we infer Prufrock's (or Eliot's) insecurity about his own existential, bodily awkwardness. It is the waiter's awkwardness—the waiter who finds himself ever the unparticipating, excluded spectator.

Although Prufrock determines to "walk upon the beach," which rhymes cheaply with "peach" and with "mermaids singing, each to each," the mermaids remain aloof and inaccessible: "I do not think that they will sing to me." Mermaids are not wooed by cloying rhymes. "They are a source of torture for Prufrock, an aging man of imagination who has heard the call of the sirens, but has not had the courage to answer," as Wendy Steiner pithily puts it.[12] Prufrock's strolling on the beach in white flannel trousers recalls Benjamin's urban *flâneur*, "an incipient version of the bourgeois consumer who endows objects with an imaginary exchange value."[13] A peach for a mermaid.

Because of his insatiable voyeuristic interests, Prufrock exemplifies the waiter who always suspects that he, too, is intensely scrutinized, and which suspicion provokes the waiter's characteristic self-consciousness about his objectification: "(They will say: 'How his hair is growing thin! ... 'how his arms and legs are thin!')" and later on: "Shall I part my hair behind? Do I dare to eat a peach?" Unlike Marvell's speaker, who strappingly proposes to "at once our time devour, / Than languish in his slow-chapped power," Prufrock, who will not consummate his desire even for a sensuous peach, fidgets, fusses, squirms, and twiddles, through one hundred thirty-one lines, and only at the end when he lies about having lingered in his intimate version of the Lacanian imaginary—"We have lingered in the chambers of the sea / By sea-girls wreathed with seaweed"—he drowns in the prattling din of some Victorian drawing room in some part of London.

Although the word *linger* occurs first in line eighteen—ominously associated with smog—and then again at the very end of the poem as an unconsummated, thwarted experience, Prufrock can no more act than he can linger. His deficiencies seem to exemplify what Nick Yablon has described as "older skills of time reckoning" that for Prufrock have ostensibly atrophied.[14] To put this differently, Prufrock suffers at once from a Baudelairian *spleen* where "the perception of time is supernaturally keen" and from a Bergsonian *durée* that "has the miserable endlessness of a scroll," to borrow Benjamin's felicitous comments on Baudelaire.[15] Homeless in time, Prufrock cannot make his home in duration.

The weariness of waiting

The consumption of objects is to compensate for the waste and worthless time wherein we wait. My sensual, mental, or visual absorption in things—peaches, teacups, skirts trailing along the floor, arms braceleted or bare—promises a brief but relatively secluded material refuge from the humiliations of waiting. Each thing is to be consumed so that time does not consume me. Each is a substitute for a time that does not have to be endured. Each thing in the waiter's eye briefly takes its turn as a substitute for the elusive, final thing waited for. If my waiting always seems endless, a *thing* puts an end to this endlessness and heals the injuries sustained by my waiting—but only briefly, for a thing's temporality is the speed of its consumption.

In Prufrock's endless cups, marmalade, tea, and porcelain; in the cluttered pages of *People* magazine (to which my scholarly wife inexplicably subscribes); in the interminable facts, figures, and fantasies of our electronic media, we will ever have to die another death in another thing. The inexhaustible supply of anesthesia is meant to assure us that we need not wake up. The temporality of things is ideologically constructed and economically administered. Since we want things, and since we want them *now*, the supply of useful things as substitutions for the uselessness of waiting is to be as endless and inexhaustible as the time that the thing replaces. The market that will never be saturated is not spatial or geographic but temporal. And the waiter's consciousness in this temporal economy exhibits a particular neurosis. She waits when she consumes things without wanting them. Or vice-versa, she consumes things without wanting them when she waits. The not-wanting-of-waiting has now been displaced into the not-knowing-of-consuming. As a result, the things that we consume unconsciously while we wait will be eminently forgettable, and if forgettable then replaceable, and if replaceable then the demand for such goods will be insatiable. Imposed and lengthened periods of waiting not only boost the economics of consumption but they also, by the logic of subject–object reversibility, alienate the waiter from himself, for he is subject to the things that consume him as much as they are subject to his consuming. I wait and gain weight.

The waiter's choice of the things he consumes while he waits, as I'm suggesting, is only seemingly deliberate. It is precisely because I think that I am briefly *not* subject to the constraints of waiting when I open another bag of lightly salted pretzels, it is precisely because my autonomy is illusory, that my consumption of things—cups of tea, pretzels, skirts—turns out to be capricious, random, unpredictable, and thus eminently subject to commercial manipulation. Not only is the waiter's autonomy in the choices he makes illusory, but it is also illusory to assume that the particular thing he thinks he consumes is not the boringly generic. We have known the arms already, known them all. Indeed, the fastidious particularity of the *braceleted* arms or the *lightly* salted pretzels only conceals the generic, repeatable, and thus forgettable quality of each thing that takes its turn to distract the waiter from his endurance of time. In sum, because our waiting has no end, and because we avoid waiting at any cost, the consumption of things is unconscious and compulsive, and our appetite for them insatiable.

The economics of waiting supports and maintains the smooth functioning of capitalism and its social stratifications. Its purpose is subtly monitored and manipulated. When Byung-Chul Han in his book *The Scent of Time: A Philosophical Essay on the Art of Lingering*, deplores that "today we are unable to linger" and later on, "In the consumer society, one forgets how to linger,"[16] we might wonder whether this development is perhaps wholly profitable to the powers that be. To that effect, Stewart points out "that violence is less able to erupt from individuals when they have submitted their agency to the time system and committed themselves to its reproduction through their everyday lives."[17] Indeed, such are the lives of the punctual and dependable; such are the lives of those who wait. They live everyday lives. They have forgotten how to linger.

When waiting is endured in public, in waiting rooms, lobbies, airports, or supermarkets, in queues, and numbers, the weariness of waiting is communally shared. It is virtuous. It fosters patience. It keeps you in place. The name of "patient Job" is proverbially invoked and piously attached to waiting. But waiting is also loathed. It fosters impatience. It is universally thought to be a waste of time. It consolidates corrupt political and social structures. These contradictions themselves effect a useful paralysis such that waiting, like no other activity, contributes to a universal if necessarily unhappy social consensus. Even the rich, while waiting for their dividends, also wait for death; everybody waits. Nobody likes it.

Notes

1 Berger, *About Looking*, 108.
2 My use of the noun, the waiter, for the person who waits is, of course, intentional. As a professional designation for the server or host in a restaurant, the term emphasizes the subservient position of the person who waits.
3 Martin Luther King, Jr. *A Testament of Hope: The Essential Writings and Speeches of Martin Luther King, Jr.* (New York: Harper Collins, 1991), 523.
4 Friedrich Nietzsche, *The Dawn of Day,* trans. John F. McFarland Kennedy (New York: MacMillan, 1911), 5.
5 King, *A Testament of Hope*, 292.
6 Harold Schweizer, *On Waiting* (London: Routledge, 2008).
7 Lars Svendsen, *A Philosophy of Boredom*, trans. John Irons (London: Reaktion Books, 2005), 127.
8 Bergson, *Duration and Simultaneity* in *Key Writings*, 206.
9 Eliot, *The Complete Poems and Plays*, 15.
10 Andrew Marvell, *The Complete Poems* (Harmondsworth: Penguin Books, 1976), 51.
11 For this reading I am gratefully indebted to Saundra Morris.
12 Wendy Steiner, *The Scandal of Pleasure: Art in an Age of Fundamentalism* (Chicago: U of Chicago P, 1995), 135.
13 Alexander Gelley, *Benjamin's Passages: Dreaming, Awakening* (New York: Fordham UP, 2015), 118.
14 Nick Yablon, "Untimely Objects: Temporal Studies and the New Materialism" in Allen, 128.
15 Benjamin, *Illuminations*, 184–185.

16 Byung-Chul Han, *The Scent of Time: A Philosophical Essay on the Art of Lingering* (London: Polity P, 2017), 31, 75.
17 Stewart, *Poetry and the Fate of the Senses*, 224; referencing Norbert Elias's book *Time: An Essay.*

4 The poet's idleness

The lingering of being

In *The Arcades Project*, Walter Benjamin notes that for Plato and Aristotle, the idle were privileged over tradesmen and artisans, and that in the Middle Ages "the contemplative man remains immobile at the center [of the wheel of fortune]."[1] While the leisure of the poet in feudal society, Benjamin goes on, "is a recognized privilege," in bourgeois society, "the poet becomes an idler."[2] Since the nineteenth century, the poet has suffered this wholly dubious designation. A poet merely muses and dallies. "I sit upon this old grey stone, / And dream my time away," Wordsworth declares.[3] Keats confesses in his "Ode to a Nightingale" that "a drowsy numbness pains / My sense, as though of hemlock I had drunk."[4] Whitman announces near the beginning of "Song of Myself," "I loafe and invite my soul, / I lean and loafe at my ease observing a spear of summer grass."[5] One could find many more examples of such idle, slightly inebriated, occupation, especially in the Romantic tradition. Since then, the poet can be held no more accountable for what happens in his poem than the idle can be held accountable for daydreaming. Perhaps daydreaming, idling, and lingering predispose one to become a poet. Perhaps poets are merely lazy. It must be easy to be a poet. Having proverbially too much time on their hands, leaning and loafing at their ease, the idle appear to commit themselves to no time system. Lingering seems purposeless and irrelevant except for poets who have drunk of hemlock or observe spears of summer grass.

Nor does Benjamin's authoritative reference to the God of Creation absolve the idler from the charge of passive collusion with social and political conservatism: while "It is this God of the seventh day that the bourgeois has taken as the model for his idleness," he adds in another aphorism, "how deeply idleness is marked by features of the capitalist economic order in which it flourishes."[6] Cioran ironically comments on such association when he says that while the idle are "born into an eternal Sunday," they "imitate the others ... to indulge in the degrading temptation of tasks. This is the danger which threatens sloth, that miraculous residue of paradise."[7] Benjamin's and Cioran's references to Genesis echo the German Romantic Friedrich Schlegel who in his "*Idylle über den Müßiggang*" (Idyll about Idling) (1799) declares that "industry and utility, are the angels of death who with fiery sword forbid man's return to paradise."[8] But the degrading temptation of tasks Cioran is speaking of is not openly imposed on the idle by the villainous forces of capitalism but more nefariously and surreptitiously by the idle themselves whose manufactured desire wrests the fiery swords from the angels and compulsively reproduces the hegemony of capitalism. Am I guilty of such compulsion by writing this book in my retirement? Should we all become Romantic poets? Are we unable to linger today? Have we forgotten how to linger?

In an interview with *Le Monde-Dimanche* about laziness, Roland Barthes regrets that the Parisian concierges no longer sit on warm evenings in front of their apartment buildings "doing nothing. It's an image of idleness that has disappeared. I don't see it anymore .... In modern Paris, there aren't as many gestures of idleness."[9] "Now, more than at any other time in history," Stewart deplores, "we seem likely to lose touch with the realm of nondetermined, we might say 'nondedicated,' time and space ... because of the relentless purging of boredom from our everyday existence."[10] No less pessimistic, Han warns that "The acceleration of life in general robs the human being of the capacity for contemplation." When he goes on to say that, "Thus, those things which only reveal themselves in contemplative lingering remain hidden,"[11] we might ask not only what those mysterious things are that remain so annoyingly hidden, but also why they should not remain hidden or what the value of such hidden things might be to deserve disclosure and attention. Such questions, of course, underlie the very status of the humanities in our time. They are as suspect and useless as poetry. What could it be that we are missing? Why should we learn to linger? What is it that remains hidden in our accelerated lives? Han offers an insightful answer with reference to Heidegger's philosophy of time:

> Heidegger's "being" has a temporal aspect: "Whiling," "tarrying," "perpetuating," is the old sense of the word "being." Only being permits lingering, because it "whiles" and "perpetuates" (*weilt und währt*). Thus, the age of haste and acceleration is an age of forgetfulness of being.[12]

So, the mysterious hidden thing is the most obvious thing; it is hidden in plain sight. It is mere being—our being of which we are forgetful and negligent. I don't see it anymore writes Barthes; we seem likely to have lost touch, writes Stewart; the acceleration of life has robbed us of our being. It is in the art of lingering, Han's book argues, that we rediscover it.

Since there is an art to lingering "because it 'whiles' and 'perpetuates,'" as the title of Han's book, *The Scent of Time: A Philosophical Essay on the Art of Lingering*, announces, it is not surprising that lingering has to be learned—I should say re-learned, since, as Bachelard points out, lingering is an essential aspect of childhood. If we live in an "age of haste," we realize that most of us willfully or unintentionally fail to relearn lingering. And if our very being depends on the hidden thing that reveals itself only to one who lingers—Whitman's "smallest sprout," for example,[13]—a thing so inconspicuous, Heidegger calls it *das Geringe*, the small, the unimportant—then its neglect diminishes our own existence. Seeing a small, hidden thing in a contemplative gaze, seeing in it an allegory of our own being, Heidegger implies, is an existential self-affirmation. Even if boredom—purged from our frantic, electronic, wired lives—may be an involuntary component of lingering, it is in boredom, for example, that we might perform such acts of attention—not because we so choose when we are bored but perhaps because we are accidentally distracted from surfing or texting or eating potato chips. Lars Svensen writes in his book *A Philosophy of Boredom* that "For Heidegger, boredom is a privileged fundamental mood because it leads us directly into the very problem complex of being and time."[14]

The hopelessness of lingering

Vladimir and Estragon wait in *Waiting for Godot*. We linger in the play because we know that Godot won't come, while the play's first audiences waited for Godot and wanted their money back. The confusion between waiting and lingering is experienced by our students who when assigned the reading of *Waiting for Godot* might find themselves sorely waiting for it to end when they should learn to linger, perhaps twice, in the play's two acts. In such an unlikely event, their *lingering* might reveal the different temporality of *waiting* endured by Beckett's characters. The pleasures of lingering might impart to the student the empathy to glimpse the misery of Vladimir and Estragon's waiting. If the play were performed for prison inmates with life sentences or patients of a hospice, they in turn might recognize that Vladimir and Estragon wait like them, without hope.

Although lingering is not waiting, lingering is hopeless. But it is not equal to hopeless waiting. The temporality of lingering, as we have said, is the present; the temporality of hope is the future. In "East Coker," Eliot ponders such a temporality without teleology and futurity. When the speaker exhorts his soul to "wait without hope," he invokes not a hopeless waiting but a waiting without future, object, or desire: "...the faith and the love and the hope are all in the waiting"[15]—which is to say faith, love, and hope are lived and embodied; their temporality in Eliot's poem is the present. Eliot may well have had Emerson's observation in "Self Reliance" in mind: "When good is near you, when you have life in yourself.... Fear and hope are alike beneath it."[16] A Heideggerian thought.

If the soul is *lived* not thought, *embodied* not imagined, it is not an article of faith (or hope) but a pound of flesh, so to speak. It is a temporality. The soul lingers. Its natural rhythm, its duration, as we shall see in Whitman's poetry, is the body. The person who lingers is, unbeknownst to her, spiritually inclined. Duration, as Merleau-Ponty succinctly puts this, "is the milieu in which soul and body find their articulation because the present and the body, the past and the mind...pass into one another."[17]

The suspension of the object waited for in *Waiting for Godot*, like the suspension of hope in "East Coker," offers helpful paradigms for the writing or reading of poetry. No poet waits for the end of her poem. Nothing need be waited for outside the closure of the poem. Nothing can be waited for in the poem. Nor does the end of a poem conclude our reading of it. A poem is the answer to its question. A poem has no teleology. The last stanza of Keats's "Ode to a Nightingale" calls him back to the beginning of the poem. The first stanza of his "Ode on a Grecian Urn" announces the inviolable temporality of the urn's "slow time."[18] When Wordsworth exclaims in "Tintern Abbey," "Therefore am I still / A lover of the meadows and the woods, / And mountains,"[19] he tells us that his poem has no end, for each reading transfers unto the reader the continuity of loving. Even Coleridge's dejection that imperils the writing of his poem transforms into the very poem imperilled by the dejection, so that the title "Dejection: An Ode" announces the ode as cure of the very dejection it bemoans: "to be still and patient" is accomplished by the poem's "abstruse research" which in turn shapes salubriously "the habit of my soul."[20] The self-sufficiency of the temporality of lingering here traced in the autonomy of poetic rhetoric is exemplified in Emily Dickinson's poem whose sexual allusions are but thinly veiled:

32   The poet's idleness

> To make a prairie it takes a clover and a bee,
> One clover, and a bee,
> And revery.
> The revery alone will do,
> If bees are few.[21]

A poem is a composition of revery, of lingering, of idling. The idling poet needs an idling reader. If lingering can't be ordered or required, one can't be ordered or required to read a poem. One doesn't linger *for* something. Like the poem, lingering has no teleology. Literary (or spiritual) readings should be done lingeringly—not waitingly. The poem speaks in one's lingering. One should look at paintings lingeringly. One should listen to music lingeringly. One should read with one's soul. No wonder that when Emerson opens his eyes in his sunny spot, he lets what would pass through them into the soul. One should do no more than take one's time to enter the time of the poem. When Whitman invites his reader, "Loafe with me on the grass," one doesn't loaf through "Song of Myself" like the urban *flâneur* for the imaginary exchange value of a meaning or a good grade. If such a value were expected, one would almost certainly have been found marching. Bodily and mental movements such as strolling, meandering, wandering, rambling—and their less sprightly variations of lingering, loafing or whiling away—have their values in themselves; they are kin to poetry—a kinship made famous by the idling Romantics—Thoreau, Emerson, Whitman, Dickinson, Wordsworth, Keats, Coleridge, and others. Maurice Blanchot thinks of poems as detours: "prose, a continuous line; verse, an interrupted line that turns about in a coming and going"[22]—and which turns and comings and goings of poetic lines Gerald Bruns has called "ecstatic time."[23] Such is the "slow time" of the Grecian urn in Keats's ode. Such was the idling of the concierges in Barthes' Paris.

A poem is not a train station. We linger in a poem. The sign *"No Loitering"* affixed to the door of the waiting room at the bus station in Harrisburg, Pennsylvania literalizes the difference between waiting and lingering. A book of poetry invites loitering. Train or bus stations are made for waiting, not loitering. They are made to be left. If we nonetheless buy a volume of Keats's odes in the bus station instead of a bag of potato chips (an unlikely scenario), we enter a different temporality wherein reading subsumes waiting, wherein the empty *quantity* of time is perchance transformed into a tranquil *quality*. One sees no more one's relation, how near and petty, to this town or that; one heeds no more what minute or hour our official clocks might indicate. "[A] real book needs real time," writes Jeanette Winterson, "and only by paying that small courtesy can a reader begin to unravel it...haste in the writer, haste in the reader, and haste is the enemy of art."[24] The more deliberate, the slower the reading, the less are we, quite paradoxically, subject to time. The slower the reading the longer the book. Books are not made to be left. Though in the meantime, one might have missed the bus.

Notes

1 Benjamin, *The Arcades Project*, 800. In *Metaphysics* Aristotle argues that the arts directed to recreation are "wiser... because their branches of knowledge did not aim at utility" (I, I, 17–19).
2 Ibid., 805.
3 Wordsworth, *William Wordsworth*, 130.
4 John Keats, *The Poems of John Keats* (London: Heinemann, 1978), 369.
5 Whitman, *Complete Poetry and Collected Prose*, 27.
6 Benjamin, *The Arcades Project*, 805.
7 Cioran, *A Short History of Decay*, 23.
8 Friedrich Schlegel, "Idylle über den Müßiggang" in *Kritische Friedrich-Schlegel-Ausgabe*. Vol. 5. (München: Holzinger, 1962), 26; my trans.
9 Roland Barthes, *The Grain of the Voice: Interviews 1962–1980*, trans. Linda Coverdale (Berkeley: U of California P, 1991), 341.
10 Stewart, *The Poet's Freedom*, 201.
11 Han, *The Scent of Time*, 59.
12 Ibid., 61.
13 Whitman, *Complete Poetry and Collected Prose*, 194.
14 Svendsen, *A Philosophy of Boredom*, 116.
15 Eliot, *The Complete Poems and Plays*, 180.
16 Emerson, "Self Reliance" in *Emerson's Prose and Poetry*, 129.
17 Merleau-Ponty, *Signs*, 185.
18 Keats, *The Poems of John Keats*, 372.
19 Wordsworth, *William Wordsworth*, 134.
20 *The Norton Anthology of English Literature: The Romantic Period*, ed. Stephen Greenblatt (New York: W.W. Norton & Company, 2006), 468.
21 *The Poems of Emily Dickinson*, ed. R.W. Franklin (Cambridge: The Belknap P of Harvard UP, 1999), # 1779.
22 Maurice Blanchot, *The Infinite Conversation*, trans. Susan Hanson (Minneapolis: U of Minnesota P, 1993), 30.
23 Gerald L. Bruns. *Maurice Blanchot: The Refusal of Philosophy* (Baltimore: Johns Hopkins UP, 1997), 123.
24 Jeanette Winterson, *Art Objects: Essays on Ecstasy and Effrontery* (London: Vintage, 1996), 89–90.

5 The ecstasy of slowness

The stillness of the Sabbath

In his collection of aphorisms, *Minima Moralia*, Adorno claims that "The gaze that loses itself on a single beautiful object, is a Sabbatical one. It salvages in the object something of the stillness of its day of creation." It is in the temporality of lingering (*Tempo des Verweilens*), Adorno argues, that the singular beautiful (*das eine Schöne*) emerges from its hiddenness among the obliterating mass of the general. If we were to linger, tarry, dwell—if our gaze were to assume the quiet stillness that Adorno coins the Sabbath gaze—we would do justice to a singular object that would thereby come to light.[1] But the gaze must *lose* itself in its object. Only the losing will disclose the beautiful.

The word *lose* announces a reflective stillness; it intimates that the Sabbath gaze is not premeditated, calculated, or even intentional. It is the innocence of the gaze that salvages in the object the stillness (*Ruhe*) of the day of its creation. The word *Ruhe*, stillness, quiet, rest, implies both an auditory quiet and a lingering slowness of movement, above all the movement of the sensory apparatus that wants to consume all things. It is in my stillness, in the slowness of my lingering, in the lingering of my gaze, that the beautiful can manifest itself. If the Sabbath is the day *par excellence* wherein the creator *rests*, and because of this resting finds her creation beautiful, then crustaceans, foliage on wallpaper, *designs à la grèque*,[2] a spear of summer grass, breath, armpits (Whitman adds), indeed anything—and we are things too—invites, indeed necessitates, Sabbatical readings.

Like the beautiful, the stillness of the Sabbath is intrinsic. Neither has economic purpose. Before we used "to indulge in the degrading temptation of tasks," to recall Cioran, such as mowing our lawns, shopping at Walmart, grading papers, or driving our kids to the soccer game, the Sabbath was supposed to be a guarantor of social equality since ideally all competition and economic consumption rests on that day. And quite to that point, as Dieter Bonhoeffer writes in his *Breviary*, the Sabbath rest (*Feiertagsruhe*) is to be kept so that we would not succumb to the illusion that it is our work that sustains us.[3]

Nothing is bartered, wanted, or won on the Sabbath. "Apart from the pulling and hauling stands what I am," writes Whitman.[4] For Whitman, any day of the week is a Sabbath day. It is the day on which one "bends an arm on an impalpable certain rest"; it is the day on which "[t]he farmer stops by the bars ... on a First-day loafe and looks at the oats and rye";[5] it is there for observing, waiting *on* and witnessing of that which was "dropt" during the week: "the handkerchief of the Lord," for example. The Sabbath gaze that rests on the sudden exquisite particularity of a single spear of summer grass, or a single poem, or a handkerchief is to assure no more, Whitman declares, than "that we may see and remark, and say *Whose?*"[6] The answer is, God's. For the beautiful is dropt; it happens; it befalls the mind like grace.

In his aphorism on the Sabbath gaze, Adorno suggests a temporal paradigm by which we inhabit simultaneously and not without vexation both materialist and idealist, both economic and aesthetic ideologies. Adorno is enough of an economist himself to understand that attention to a singular constitutes an injustice to the general, that eventually there must be a transfer of attention, a *Weise des Übergangs*,[7] from the particular to the general, from the singular to the social, from the personal to the historical. In this transfer of attention, we conceptualize, contextualize, situate, and communicate the particular, to which, however, by attending to the general, we commit the injustice of generalization and stereotyping. The truth that reveals itself in beholding a singular object, to paraphrase Adorno, constitutes an injustice towards the general, but without committing this injustice, no singular thing will reveal itself. But yet again, since "no particular aesthetic experience occurs in isolation," as Adorno insists in *Aesthetic Theory*,[8] since the relationship between the particular and the universal is always dialectical, we restlessly, yet necessarily, alternate, oscillate, or shuttle back and forth (as I have been doing in this paragraph) like the pendulum of a clock, between the poles of this dialectic.

What Adorno *the aesthete* therefore proposes—and I think this is the gist of his advocacy of slowness—is to slow the movement of this pendulum between the particular and the general. Rendering justice to the singular, he declares, is a matter of *Tempo, der Geduld und Ausdauer des Verweilens*,[9] a matter of speed, patience, and endurance of lingering, before the singular is eventually erased in the general concept. Adorno calls the abuse by which such processes of erasure are performed as *Gedanken als Gewalt*, thinking as violence and *Abkürzen des Wegs*,[10] shortcut of the process. Works of art resist such shortcuts. Blanchot, as we have seen, thinks of poems as detours. "The detour," he insists, "is not a shortcut ... It is a matter of holding to it, holding up and keeping up."[11]

To *behold* a spear of summer grass, or to read a poem, then, is a function of holding up, of slowness—such as is elicited by the undulating rhythms of Whitman's lines, for example, or by the "slow time" of Keats's Grecian urn, or by the dreamy length of Proust's sentences, or by Virginia Woolf's sensuous syntax, or by W.G. Sebald's melancholic reveries, as much as by the ceremonious formality of a sonnet, or the fragile, fleeting gesture of a flower,[12] or the nuanced forms and colors of a painting—the latter, incidentally, according to Jacques Lacan, requiring a "taming," "civilizing," and "seducing" of the eyes' "voracity."[13] Even an unlikely butterfly can effect such seducing as Wordsworth notes in "To a Butterfly," "I've watched you now a full half hour, / Self-poised upon that yellow flower."[14]

Wordsworth's blissful enchantment in that poem suggests that a miraculous residue of paradise clings to the slowness of "a full half hour." Like Adorno, the German philosopher Hans-Georg Gadamer claims that we learn from the work of art how to linger, *verweilen*, a word, as we have seen, also used by Adorno, and that in this lingering the work of art affords us a glimpse of "what one might call eternity."[15] The verb *to while away* echoes the German *verweilen*, especially in its explicit temporal qualifier—*to while away one's time*. The slightly more tranquil, elongated temporality of the word *verweilen* resonates with Gadamer's sense of an eternity, while he who *whiles* in English seems either innocently or recklessly to *fritter away* his time. The minuscule trace of waste and sloth that clings to the English expression and its allusion to squandering is wholly absent in German. And yet, common to both languages is that the temporalities of waiting and lingering, as we have noted, seem to be mutually exclusive: she who lingers does not wait; he who waits does not linger. One is told to wait; one can't be told to linger; many Romantic poems gently invite us to linger. One often likes to linger; one rarely likes to wait. If lingering is ritualized or imposed, as Barthes points out, "it becomes torture. This torture is called boredom."[16]

Slow reading

We linger between haste and boredom. Neither haste nor boredom, lingering is slowness: hence strolling, wandering, reflecting, contemplating, dwelling upon, dawdling, savoring. Reading, which we once might have thought is going straight to the point, is slowness. Pleasure, which we once might have thought is going straight to the point, is slowness. In *The Pleasure of the Text*, Barthes defines bad reading as skipping, good reading as skipping nothing; bad reading as missing out on the play of language, good reading as reading "with application and transport ... the layering of significance." We read with haste, Barthes claims, because we want to avoid being bored. "Read slowly," he concludes, and the text will come alive "in the uttering, not in the sequence of utterances: not to devour, to gobble, but to graze, to browse scrupulously, to rediscover."[17] Barthes' metaphors of voracity for fast reading versus lingering for slow reading suggest that the latter not only resembles the leisurely savoring of a meal—one doesn't scarf down a poem—but that slow reading stimulates and develops taste—the very word Kant uses for the judgment of the beautiful. Slowness begets the beautiful; the beautiful begets gratitude.

In the fifth aphorism of *Daybreak*, Nietzsche—who admired Emerson, while Barthes admired Nietzsche—famously defines philology as the art of slow reading:

> I have not been a philologist in vain—perhaps I am one yet: a teacher of slow reading. I even come to write slowly. At present it is not only my habit, but even my taste—a perverted taste, maybe—to write nothing but what will drive to despair everyone who is "in a hurry." For philology is that venerable art which exacts from its followers one thing above all—to step to one side, to leave themselves spare moments, to grow silent, to become slow—the leisurely art of the goldsmith applied to language: an art which must carry out slow, fine work, and attains nothing if not *lento*. For this very reason philology is now more desirable than ever before; for this very reason it is the highest attraction and incitement in an age of "work": that is to say, of haste, of unseemly and immoderate hurry-skurry, which is intent upon "getting things done" at once, even every book, whether old or new. Philology itself, perhaps, will not "get things done" so hurriedly: it teaches how to read *well: i.e.* slowly, profoundly, attentively, prudently, with inner thoughts, with the mental doors ajar, with delicate fingers and eyes ... my patient friends, this book appeals only to perfect readers and philologists: *learn* to read me well![18]

One is to stand beside oneself (the etymological meaning of the Greek *ek-stasis*), be beside oneself; one is "to step to one side, to leave oneself spare moments, to grow silent, to become slow." One is to proceed "slowly, profoundly, attentively, prudently, with inner thoughts, with the mental doors ajar, with delicate fingers and eyes." In the first instance Nietzsche defines slowness by verbs, in the second by adverbs—which amounts to saying that slowness, like lingering, is active. It is an activity not a passivity. Or, if it is a passivity, it is, to recall Stewart, a vigilant passivity. It is also secretly oppositional, even defiant, perhaps even ecstatic—implied in Barthes' word "transport" (*emportement*) by which one is carried away.

Nietzsche's advocacy for slow reading offers resistance to what Boulous Walker in her book *Slow Philosophy: Reading against the Institution* has called dominant institutional modes of reading and teaching predicated on speed, efficiency, closure, knowledge, mastery. Institutional modes of reading are based on the temporality and teleology of waiting—waiting for the next sentence, the next page, the end, the meaning, the grade, the graduation—whereas *slow* reading implies the suspension, even the subversion, of those aims. There are thus two temporalities in the formula *slow reading*: 1.) the linear, sequential, mechanical, goal-oriented process of reading disrupted 2.) by the slowness of meandering, retrospection, re-reading, speculation, doubt, criticism. It is easier to read fast than slowly. It is easier to rush than to wait. It is easier to wait than to linger. Waiting is imposed—all one has to do is obey, while lingering is voluntary—it requires inclination and initiative. It requires, to repeat Proust's phrase, "the mind to work upon itself."[19] If an education in literary reading should be an education in slow reading, we can perhaps appreciate the effort it takes to acquire such an education. For everything in our age of haste seems to be opposed to slowness and thus to literature and thus to a humanistic education—and thus to beauty and gratitude.

Slowness is an activity. For it is by slowness that we make meaning. The making of meaning unfolds on the level of minute particulars—for example, as *I read or write this sentence*. The meaning of the word "read" in this sentence comes about through space, i.e., its visible difference from other words, like "write," and it comes about through time, i.e., the deferral by which this space between "read" and "write" is traversed. This difference and deferral, of space and time, conjoin, as we know, in what Jacques Derrida has coined *différance*. A word means what it means because of *différance*, because of difference and deferral. We can thus say that *différance* is a function of a very carefully calibrated slowness. If I read too quickly, the deferral is erased—*read or write* blend into each other—if I read too slowly, the difference is erased—and the word *read* stands out, orphaned and solitary, like the weird sound that the word [ree: d] is. *Différance*, which is to say, how we make meaning, is thus, I suggest, a matter of lingering. I have to linger in my sentence. In his analysis of historical temporality, Jean Baudrillard puts a very fine point on this process of difference and deferral:

> A degree of slowness (that is, a certain speed, but not too much), a degree of distance, but not too much, and a degree of liberation (an energy for rupture and change), but not too much, are needed to bring about the kind of condensation or significant crystallization of events we call history, the kind of coherent unfolding of causes and effects we call reality (*le réel*).
> Once beyond this gravitational effect, which keeps bodies in orbit, all the atoms of meaning get lost in space.[20]

When Georg Lukács considers how time runs its course in a novel, we realize that he thinks of novels as a *slow* reader; duration, not linear clock-time, determines the form of the novel; the writer and her characters, he argues, might move in "many dimensions and no direction."[21] This multidimensional and multidirectional movement marks the narrative particularly in modernist novels as threatening to undermine the sequential, linear unfolding that structures realist novels. In avant-garde styles, we find Baudrillard's "gravitational effect" perilously close to being suspended. Despite their daunting bulk, realist novels are faster paced than modernist novels. The fact that the designation "page-turner" is meant as a compliment reveals our preference for speed over slowness.

For Lukács time masters form, which implies the form of the novel has to be supple and elastic, even porous, to accommodate the multidimensional and multidirectional movements of the characters, and the inner thoughts and mental doors that might blow a gentle drought into the idea of condensation, crystallization, efficiency, sequence, logic, meaning, closure, and good grades. In a summary or paraphrase by contrast—which one consults to get things done and make a hundred dollars—only the linear sequence is present, while the inner thoughts are simplistically subdued or censored, and the half-open doors are resolutely shut. It is thus, among some other differences, in its temporality, its slowness, that a literary text differs from a vacuum cleaner manual. The velocity of a vacuum cleaner manual is veritably precipitous compared to the meandering pace of Keats's "Ode to a Nightingale."

If "to read *well*," as Nietzsche proposes, is to read "slowly, profoundly, attentively, prudently, with inner thoughts," we recognize that Emerson's lingering in a sunny spot between Boston and Cambridge—indeed much of the lingering I consider here—participates in and is engendered by the same gentle, deliberate, concentrated mental activity that Nietzsche calls slow reading.

Time's unfolding

Bergson's concept of time as duration is not so different from Nietzsche's concept of slow reading. In *The Creative Mind*, Bergson recalls an event that had occurred 50 years earlier: "one fine day" during his philosophic ruminations about the evolutionary philosopher Herbert Spencer, Bergson observed that in Spencer's philosophy "time served no purpose, did nothing. Nevertheless I said to myself, time is something. Therefore it acts. What can it be doing?" The answer he gives implies that the kind of slowness Nietzsche advocates transports us into a profound alignment with the nature of time itself: "[T]ime," Bergson explains,

> is what hinders everything from being given at once. It retards, or rather it is retardation. It must, therefore, be elaboration. Would it not then be a vehicle for creation and choice? Would not the existence of time prove that there is indetermination in things? Would not time be that indetermination itself?[22]

While skipping, skimming, summarizing, abridging, and condensing all aim to produce what can be "given at once," slow reading attunes itself to time's unfolding, in which unfolding there is the potential for creation and choice. "One must be an inventor to read well," Emerson writes in "The American Scholar." "There is then creative reading as well as creative writing."[23] Sadly, we encourage our students not to be Emersonian inventors but laborers intent on getting things done in a dehumanizing age of work.

Evidently, Bergson's insight into the necessary alignment of creativity and temporality arrived neither "at once," nor by squinting philosophic speculation, but merely fortuitously, "one fine day," during which Bergson is said to have whiled away his time reading Spencer, at first dejectedly thinking that "time served no purpose, did nothing" but in the slow unfolding of time mirrored in his syntax—reconsidered his assumption. The "fine day" on which he performed these cogitations was a slow day; or rather it was a slow day *because* he performed such cogitations. While the lingering that retards is in harmony with time that retards, Bergson's own thinking on that fine day as well as over the span of 50 years, as well as in that very paragraph ending with three questions that hold its determination in abeyance (albeit rhetorically)—implies his own lingering over these questions and his embodied harmony with the duration he describes as elaboration and creation. Like time, his thinking is elaborating, unfolding. Like time, it is not given at once. It is slow. Above all, both time and lingering act, they are actions, and the indeterminacy of time is mirrored and embodied in the indeterminacy of Bergson's philosophic lingering. It is creative to linger.

Slow time

Poems compose a temporality that slows time; by slowing, time expands; within its expansion, time elaborates. When we read slowly, we experience such delays and expansions as calm or repose. Let me name this calm *lyric time*. Although a vacuum cleaner manual is usually not read in the calm of lyric time, *literary* prose can be read in lyric time, as I will try to show below and in my readings of Woolf, Proust, and Sebald.

The lyric is brief, its time is slow, but it is as expansive as Gadamer's eternity. A residue of paradise clings to the lyric; it retains the stillness of the Sabbath day. The short lyric poem also exemplifies Adorno's notion of the particular; it therefore necessitates Sabbatical readings. And like the particular, the poem incites the charge of irrelevance or irresponsibility towards the general. In Critchley's philosophic readings of the poetry of Wallace Stevens in *Things Merely Are*, we find such Sabbatical readings: "By attending to the meditative voice of Stevens," writes Critchley, "I think we can acquire something of the craft of this calm."[24] The verb "attending," the qualifying "I think" and "something" imply a gentle receptivity that acquires a calm.

Apropos of calm, we recall Wordsworth's sonnet beginning with the lines, "It is a beauteous Evening, calm and free; / The holy time is quiet as a Nun," or another of his sonnets, "Composed upon Westminster Bridge, September 3, 1802," where "a calm so deep" pervades the poem that the industrial grime of London is briefly purged and the city appears "All bright and glittering in the smokeless air."[25] Or we remember that "Tintern Abbey" is composed entirely in a "repose" that yields "beauteous forms" and as a consequence of those, inspires "little, nameless, unremembered acts / Of kindness and of love."[26] Calm and repose are the auditory, mental, and bodily dimensions of slow time, such as passes in Coleridge's "This Lime-Tree Bower My Prison" where the poet, resting in his garden bower after a slight injury, and remembering a previous restful solitude in the same spot, finds, like Emerson in his sunny hollow, a sudden joy in his seclusion:

> A delight
> Comes sudden on my heart, and I am glad
> As I myself were there! Nor in this bower,
> This little lime-tree bower, have I not marked

> Much that has soothed me. Pale beneath the blaze
> Hung the transparent foliage; and I watched
> Some broad and sunny leaf, and loved to see
> The shadow of the leaf and stem above
> Dappling its sunshine![27]

The first half of the poem, referring to Coleridge's imagined, even envied, outing with his friends from which his injury prevented him, is interrupted in the forty-third line by his "sudden" realization that the spectacular aesthetic pleasures they might enjoy on their walk are unexpectedly matched by the intimate vision that "[t]his little lime-tree bower" affords. The double negation, "Nor in this bower... have I not," reminds the poet of previous experiences in the same bucolic location and amplifies his appreciation for the humble provenance of the beautiful compared to his friends' "most fantastic sight" on their walk. The very smallness of the bower—metaphor for the lyric and for the poetic stanza, as it is metaphor for the slowness of time—elicits the intimate vision, exemplifying Adorno's Sabbath gaze, of a singular leaf, its shadow and stem. Proceeding from marking to soothing, from watching to loving, the increasing inwardness of the speaker's gaze implies the transformative, emphatic potential of lingering.

The same Sabbath gaze informs the narrator's experience —very similar to Coleridge's—of the early morning hues of light and shadow cast by the ornamental balustrade of his balcony in the third section of Proust's *Swann's Way*. The play of light on the stone balcony conveys

> ...like a whimsical vegetation, with a delicacy in the delineation of its slightest details that seemed to betray a painstaking consciousness, an artistic satisfaction, and with such sharp relief, such velvet in the restfulness of its dark and happy masses that in truth those broad and leafy reflections resting on that lake of sun seemed to know they were pledges of calm and happiness.[28]

Calm and happiness are not, obviously, just functions of the reflection of light, but of the writer's own reflection of the outward manifestations of an inner feeling that Proust here describes as "a sort of effort toward ... the pulsation of a hesitant ray that wished to discharge its light."[29] The temporality of the beautiful in the slow, calm harmonizing of inner and outer world—the effort and the hesitant ray—enacts itself in the very length and slowness of the sentence itself (of which I have only quoted one third); it is one of the many redemptive lyric episodes in Proust's writing.

Indeed, even amidst the slaughter and unspeakable suffering during and after the Civil War, Whitman finds such slow, lyric moments of restorative lingering. "So, still sauntering on, to the spring under the willows," he announces and proceeds to write of the stream and its gurgling, of the berries and herbs, of light and shade with the same moral inwardness as would Coleridge or Wordsworth: "How they and all grow into me ... the wild, just palpable perfume, and the dapple of leaf-shadows, and all the natural-medicinal, elemental-moral influences of the spot."[30] On another occasion, after a slow, beautifully detailed, painterly description of the autumn sky, Whitman apostrophizes, "Hast Thou, pellucid, in Thy azure depths, medicine for case like mine? (Ah, the physical shatter and troubled spirit of me the last three years.) And doest Thou subtly mystically now drip it through the air invisibly upon me?"[31]

"It is thus," Bachelard concludes, "that reverie demonstrates repose of the being, that reverie illustrates a state of well-being."[32] In its ecstatic slowness, in its fusing of outer and inner spaces and times, in its fleeting visitations, moments of lingering resemble lyric poems. Lyric poems are transcriptions of lingering such as Whitman proposes to the brook, "I will learn from thee, and dwell on thee—receive, copy, print from thee."[33]

The lightness of lingering

Slow reading defines the lyric not primarily as an object—morbidly, as a New Critical well-wrought urn—but as a temporality akin to "the leisurely art of the goldsmith applied to language," as Nietzsche puts it; it is "an art which must carry out slow, fine work, and attains nothing if not *lento*." It is all a learning, receiving, and dwelling on. The denigration of the lyric in our time, the deliberate rarity of poetry in the harried lives of those of us trying to get things done and make a hundred dollars, has much to do with the poem's intrinsic slowness, which is a function of Bergson's delay and elaboration, that assures that in a poem one can't get things done—either quickly or easily, nor does one get paid for it. "We have no interest," to recall Bergson again, "in listening to the uninterrupted humming of life's depth." For here time is *lento*; here time is not money; it is rather a time in which, as in "Tintern Abbey,"

> the burthen of the mystery,
> In which the heavy and the weary weight
> Of all this unintelligible world,
> Is lightened.

The association of lingering with lightness is clearly a mark of Coleridge's experience under the lime-tree bower where the near homophonous verb "delight" announces the lightness-both in the sense of weight and light—of "the transparent foliage," the "broad and sunny leaf," and the "shadow of the leaf and stem," as if in the gossamer rarity and transience of these natural objects the weary weight of the unintelligible world is briefly lifted. In "Tintern Abbey," the length of years and hours is felt as weight, but the "beauteous forms" of nature lift the "hours of weariness." A poem's slowness lightens, heals, consoles.

Notes

1 Theodor Adorno, *Minima Moralia* (Frankfurt am Main: Suhrkamp, 1982), 94; my trans.
2 Listed by Kant as objects eliciting aesthetic experiences, in *Kritik der Urteilskraft*, § 16.
3 *Bonhoeffer Brevier*, ed. Otto Dudzus (München: Kaiser Verlag, 1985), 442.
4 Whitman, *Complete Poetry and Collected Prose*, 191.
5 Ibid., 200.
6 Ibid., 193.
7 Adorno, *Minima Moralia*, 94.
8 Adorno, *Aesthetic Theory*, 268.
9 Adorno, *Minima Moralia*, 94.
10 Ibid.
11 Blanchot, *The Infinite Conversation*, 30.
12 Cf. Harold Schweizer, *Rarity and the Poetic: The Gesture of Small Flowers* (Basingstoke: Palgrave Macmillan, 2016).
13 Jacques Lacan, *Les quatre concepts fondamentaux de la psychoanalyse* (Paris: Éditions du Seuil, 1973); my trans.: "*le ressort apaisant, civilisateur et charmeur, de la fonction du tableau*" (106).
14 Wordsworth, *William Wordsworth*, 254.
15 Hans-Georg Gadamer, *Die Aktualität des Schönen*. Stuttgart: Reclam, 1977, 60; cf. also Stewart, *Poetry and the Fate of the Senses*, 204.
16 Barthes, *The Grain of the Voice*, 344.
17 Roland Barthes, *The Pleasure of the Text*, trans. Richard Miller (New York: Hill and Wang, 1975), 12.
18 Nietzsche, *The Dawn of Day*, 13–14.
19 Proust, *In the Shadow of Young Girls in Flower*, 297.
20 Jean Baudrillard, "Pataphysics of the Year 2000" in *The Jean Baudrillard Reader*, ed. Steve Redhead (Columbia UP, 2008), 125.
21 Lukács, *Die Theorie des Romans*, 108.
22 Bergson, *The Creative Mind* in *Key Writings*, 224.
23 *Emerson's Prose and Poetry*, 60.
24 Critchley, *Things Merely Are*, 89.
25 Wordsworth, *William Wordsworth*, 285.
26 Ibid.,132.

27 Greenblatt, *The Norton Anthology of English Literature: The Romantic Period*, 429.
28 Proust, *Swann's Way*, 412–413.
29 Ibid., 412.
30 Whitman, *Complete Poetry and Collected Prose,* 781–782.
31 Ibid., 793.
32 Bachelard, *On Poetic Imagination and Reverie*, trans. Colette Gaudin (Dallas: Spring Publications, Inc., 1971), 71.
33 Whitman, *Complete Poetry and Collected Prose,* 782.

6 The temporality of Whitman's grass

Loafing

The "spear of summer grass" appears in the fifth line, right at the beginning of "Song of Myself" as an emblem of the insignificant, forgettable, eminently transient thing and as an allusion to the title of the collection, *Leaves of Grass*. "All flesh is grass," we read in Isaiah, "and all the goodliness thereof is as the flower of the field. / The grass withereth, the flower fadeth: because the spirit of the Lord bloweth upon it: surely the people is grass" (40:6–7). Thus, when Whitman invites us in the opening lines of "Song of Myself," "Loafe with me on the grass…"[1] it is an invitation not only to loaf with him in the leaves of his book, but also to share his revisionist rehabilitation of us who are but grass; to grant us not reprieve from the withering breath of the Lord but to bless the very breath that withers, to celebrate our very mortality. For Whitman, the spear of summer grass is not the emblem of God's wrath but God's "handkerchief,"[2] dropped as a token of amorous courtship; it is a sign, in other words, of God's love for us who are but grass.

Unsurprisingly, Whitman's biblical heresy extends also into his poetic style: "Not words, not music or rhyme I want," he insists, "not custom or lecture, not even the best / only the lull I like.…"[3] In its smallness and insignificance, the spear of summer grass presents itself only to one who against all precepts of dogma, etiquette, and industry lulls and loafs. How different from Prufrock's anxious "Let us go then you and I." How different from Vladimir and Estragon's fretful immobility in *Waiting for Godot*. "Apart from the pulling and hauling stands what I am, / Stands amused, complacent, compassionating, idle, unitary, / …. I have no mockings or arguments," Whitman declares, "I witness and wait."[4] Whitman waits entirely without the indignities of waiting. The poem ends with the poet promising, "I stop somewhere waiting for you."[5] If the voice speaking in these lines is that of the poem and of divinity, and if the somewhere is anywhere, then we can stop anywhere in the poem, assuming—since Whitman promises at the very beginning, "what I assume you shall assume"[6]—that the poem (and God) will be waiting for us. Which is to say, the poem invites its reader to stop and linger at any point over any line or passage, beside any leaf or blade of grass, or to begin at any time. That, I assume, is the meaning of his invitation to the reader, "Loafe with me on the grass...." The poem's rhetoric is radically dialogic not monologic, its structure is rhizomatic not linear, its argument is accumulative not narrative.

> One world is aware and by far the largest to me, and that is myself,
> And whether I come to my own to-day or in ten thousand or ten million years,
> I can cheerfully take it now, or with equal cheerfulness I can wait.
> ...
> And I know the amplitude of time.[7]

"Song of Myself" contains an amplitude of 1346 lines, over which Whitman presides, as Roger Gilbert points out, "as a kind of self-declared omnipresence."[8] The poem performs a celebratory waiting, stopping, lingering, idling, sauntering, meandering, strolling, wandering, reclining and leaning; most famously a loafing. Loafing is the poor person's lingering; it is transgressive and subversive. In each of his ventures and diversions the loafer experiences "the amplitude of time," the fullness of time in which one comes into one's own, finds oneself; in which one is completed. "I exist, as I am," exclaims Whitman, "that is enough,"[9] overtly renouncing Descartes' exclusively intellectual *cogito*. In Yves Bonnefoy's essay "*Le Lieu d'herbes*," whose title allusively invokes Whitman's *Leaves of Grass*, "this place of grasses is ... present, in the sense that it is like a place where I am and not one where I should like to go or where I have been" and a little bit later on, "I am where I must be"[10]—and which congruence of will and necessity mirrors the lingerer's experience of the harmony of internal and external conditions, and of time and space.

When Whitman announces, "I lean and loafe at my ease observing a spear of summer grass,"[11] the line is not only declarative and slightly brazen, but its gangly length both performs and invites a loafing. The reader is to loaf in it. If one were to identify characteristic bodily movements or positions for the untimely temporalities we are considering here, we might assign the waiter the movement of pacing, the lingerer the position of reclining, the loafer a leaning. For the loafer lounges, lolls, and lingers, but, I imagine, he has risen from the lingerer's reclining position and leans towards some vague but extravagant intention, perhaps a strolling or a wandering. Thus, the line, "I lean and loafe at my ease observing a spear of summer grass," lounges, idles, hangs around, goes nowhere—for a moment—until the line ambles across a stanza break into the next line: "My tongue, every atom of my blood...." It is in that moment of luxurious amplitude, perhaps in the middle of the line, "I lean and loafe at my ease ... observing a spear of summer grass"—for once, in an earlier edition, Whitman had here inserted a felicitous ellipsis—it is here in hat medial caesura, I imagine, that Whitman does his witnessing and observes a spear of summer grass, just as we assume as he assumes by observing a line of poetry, as if we could linger over it, as if we could take forever to move on to the next line, as if we could say, I am where I must be.

Each of the 52 sections of "Song of Myself," each of Whitman's long, meandering lines performs a stepping to one side—an ecstasy, a standing beside oneself—apart from the pulling and hauling to leave oneself spare moments, as in Nietzsche's slow reading, as in Bergson's creative elaboration of time.

A spear of summer grass

The species of grass is a general concept. In the general concept the single spear of grass disappears. For the general implies comparability, exchangeabilty, substitution. These are economic terms, implying, as we have seen, trade, barter, haggling, dealing, and dickering, all of which suggest, were we to submit the spear of summer grass to such terms, its denigration. In the general, to put this simply, the particular is erased. In the terms of the general, what is the value of a spear of summer grass? What can I get for it? Nothing. Can I even see it unless I loaf? No, I can't. It is Whitman's purpose, of course, precisely to make economic propositions ludicrous. A spear of summer grass has no value because the only value in a time-is-money economy is exchange value. When Kafka is said to have cautioned, "let someone attempt to seize a blade of grass," which Deleuze and Guattari paraphrase as "It's not easy to see the grass in things"[12] we are reminded that it is easier to seize, hold, and keep a thing when it has the heft of a certifiable monetary value.

Whitman's verbs "observe," "witness," "wait," "lull" hold desire in abeyance, slow it down. "Tenderly will I use you curling grass," he declares (somewhat lustily).[13] Neither does he voraciously pick and devour the spear of summer grass; neither does he indifferently dis-regard it, for dis-regard would be a matter of the gaze's restlessness;

neither does the sensuous frivolity of his loafing resemble the anemic desirelessness of Kant's aesthetic; neither does it resemble the economically administered greed of the consumer of things; neither does it resemble the deferential piety of the visitor of the museum who genuflects before fetishes; nor does it resemble the satisfaction of the student of poetry whom Whitman ridicules in the rhetorical question "Have you felt so proud to get at the meaning of poems?"[14]

In observing and witnessing we do not attend to the meaning—that is to say to the mastering—of poems, for that would be to assign them exchange value. For what is mastered must serve. Whitman's radical idleness thus transgresses all the institutionalized pedagogic, economic, and moral imperatives of his day's protestant work ethic that favored, as do we, plumbers over poets. Times, alas, haven't changed. Thus, it is that erstwhile Republican presidential candidate Marco Rubio, for example, could proclaim to universal assent that "we need more welders, less philosophers" (sic).[15]

Everybody wants a welder. Nobody wants a spear of summer grass. A spear of summer grass is to be relegated to the species of grass. Once absorbed in the general, its singularity erased, its particularity anonymous, it can be mowed, trampled on, treated with toxic fertilizers, and turned into a golf course. Consider the endless analogues of such erasure of the singular in the general and the ethical implications of this erasure: What is a chicken? It is to be relegated to the anonymous species of poultry. It is therefore to be tortured and eaten. What is a cow? It is to be relegated to the anonymous species of beef. It is a steak and a handbag. And if we are good economists because we have better things to do than to look at a blade of summer grass, we should politely decline Whitman's invitation to lean and loaf with him.

And yet, if we turn the pages of *Leaves of Grass*, if we read each line as if it were a leaf of grass and each page as if it were the Lord's handkerchief, if, in other words, we accept Whitman's invitation at the beginning of "Song of Myself"—"what I assume you shall assume"— then we are compromised, inconsistent welders, golfers, carnivores, or capitalists. We see the grass in things. We have an inclination towards the beautiful. We are already leaning towards loafing.

The fetish

When the child asks, "*What is the grass?*" the answer, among the many answers Whitman attempts to give in a series of repeated guesses and maybes, is that it is eminently a thing of time and change, mystery and difference, life and death. It emerges as "the produced babe of the vegetation" and eventually transforms into "the beautiful uncut hair of graves." Thereafter Whitman's thought proceeds—not morbidly but unflinchingly—to "the hints about the dead young men and women" so that he may resurrect them in his consolatory realization that in the endless repetition of this entropic cycle "there is really no death."[16] Rather than *repressed*, death is *incorporated* in the cycle of life, symbolized in "the smallest sprout,"[17] quick, fleeting, inconspicuous like Heidegger's small thing, *das Geringe*, but discernible to the gaze of all—rabbits and loafers alike.

In Whitman's radically democratic aesthetic, anything can be beautiful: "the smoke of my own breath"; "The scent of these arm-pits aroma finer than prayer."[18] Although anemic by comparison, Kant's foremost examples for the beautiful are, more canonically, flowers; but his list, as we have noted, also includes, perhaps with gleeful seditiousness, crustaceans, *designs à la grèque*, and foliage on wallpaper.[19] For the beautiful is not a fetish but an experience, it is not timeless but temporal; it lingers; it is smoke, or a scent, or a taste.

"The false relation to art," Adorno writes in *Aesthetic Theory*, "is akin to anxiety over possession." Rather than as a "fetishistic idea of the artwork as property"[20] it is lived experience, *temps durée*, that constitutes the work of art. If haste is one way, fetishization is another to subvert the slowness by which the beautiful comes about. The temporalities of haste and fetishization are diametrically opposed. Haste is restless speed; the fetish is illusory stasis and possession. Slowness, then, is the fragile velocity between the economically administered haste and the ideologically regulated fetish. Like haste, which only accelerates the entropic flow of time in its displacements, the work of art as fetish serves as talisman against the fear of death. Whitman's opposition to the fetishizing of art is announced in the title *Leaves of Grass*, as well as in his focus on common grass—rather than Monet's elitist *Déjeuner sur l'herbe*—as the emblem of the temporal beautiful.

Raymond Williams points out "that nearly all forms of contemporary critical theory are theories of consumption. That is to say, they are concerned with understanding an object in such a way that it can profitably or correctly be consumed."[21] Of all theories of consumption, Kant's denial that anything at all is understood or consumed in the aesthetic experience seems by such measures the most ascetic—to the point that Adorno calls it "a castrated hedonism."[22] But, as Jean-François Lyotard (in a slightly different context) points out, "One cannot consume an occurrence, but merely its meaning."[23] Kant's theory is the only one, to my knowledge, in which nothing is to be consumed, everything to be experienced. The beautiful is an occurrence, an event, perhaps as inconspicuous as a small sprout. All one has to do, as I have noted, is show up. All one has to have, besides pulse, is a "leaning," an inclination, a vigilance. Moreover, while the sensuality of Kant's metaphor of taste (*Geschmack*) implies that a theory of desirelessness is thinkable only as an oxymoron, the indeterminacy of taste—explicit in the adage *de gustibus non est disputandum* (there is no disputing about taste)—felicitously renders the impossibility of its transference into consumable concept.[24]

Hence Whitman's insistence on his radically democratized aesthetics of armpits and breath. Everybody has them, welders and philosophers alike. The transference of the beautiful into consumable form and concept, of course, nonetheless occurred when the New Critics eventually remodeled Kant's aesthetic into a prodigiously productive theory of consumption once they fetishized Kantian aesthetic experience in the well-wrought urn. Although we carelessly say that somebody does or does not have taste, taste is strictly speaking democratic; it is not something one has; it is neither a possession nor a property but a brief, transient, indeterminable but perhaps entirely memorable experience.[25]

Notes

1 Whitman, *Complete Poetry and Collected Prose*, 192.
2 Ibid., 193.
3 Ibid., 192.
4 Ibid., 191–192.
5 Ibid., 247.
6 Ibid., 188, 247.
7 Ibid., 207.
8 Roger Gilbert, *Walks in the World: Representation and Experience in Modern American Poetry* (Princeton: Princeton UP, 1991), 47.
9 Whitman, *Complete Poetry and Collected Prose*, 207.
10 Bonnefoy, *The Arrière-pays*, 170, 171.
11 Whitman, *Complete Poetry and Collected Prose*, 27.
12 Gilles Deleuze und Felix Guattari, *A Thousand Plateaus: Capitalism and Schizophrenia*, trans. Brian Massumi (Minneapolis: U of Minnesota P, 1987), 23.
13 Whitman, *Complete Poetry and Collected Prose*, 193.
14 Ibid., 189.
15 *The Atlantic Monthly* (Nov. 14, 2015).
16 Whitman, *Complete Poetry and Collected Prose*, 192–194.
17 Ibid., 194.
18 Ibid., 189, 211.
19 Kant, *Kritik der Urteilskraft*, § 16.
20 Adorno, *Aesthetic Theory*, 13.
21 Raymond Williams, *Marxism and Literature* (Oxford: Oxford UP 1977), 45–46.
22 Adorno, *Aesthetic Theory*, 11.

23 Lyotard, *The Inhuman*, 80.
24 Kant, *Kritik der Urteilskraft*, § 56.
25 It is deplorable, of course, that Kant nonetheless doubted these democratic aspects of the aesthetic experience; cf. Lehman, "Lingering, Pleasure, Desire," 241, n. 34.

7 The slowness of looking

The reciprocity of the gaze

While Kant demands that in the aesthetic experience desire be altogether suspended, Adorno suggests that desire be slowed, delayed, curbed, reduced—all of which is implied in the experience of lingering. What is common to both Kant and Adorno is that the tranquility practiced in the contemplation of the work of art, and the rewards such tranquility affords, do not come about through the want and desire of the consumer of things but through the slowness of looking. The same, as we have seen, applies to slow reading.

"Aesthetic experience becomes living experience only by way of its object," Adorno maintains, but he adds a definitive temporal qualification. This only happens "in that instant in which artworks themselves become animate under its gaze."[1] For Benjamin, this reciprocity between subject and object or this animation of the object by the gaze of the beholder constitutes "the aura of an object [that] means to invest it with the ability to look at us in return."[2] In a footnote Benjamin explains that

> This endowment is a wellspring of poetry. Wherever a human being, an animal, or an inanimate object thus endowed by the poet lifts up its eyes, it draws him into the distance. The gaze of nature thus awakened dreams and pulls the poet after its dream.[3]

Although Benjamin privileges the subject's or the poet's gaze as initiating this exchange, the gaze of nature quickly casts an enchantment over the poet, drawing her into the distance, pulling her after its dream. While ostensibly echoing such Romantics as Emerson, Coleridge, Wordsworth, or Baudelaire, Benjamin's concept of reciprocity is also anticipated by another, more recent neo-Romantic, Rainer Maria Rilke.

In one of his letters to his wife Clara written from the island of Capri on March 8, 1907, Rilke adds considerable psychological depth to the reciprocity of the gaze. The experience of looking, of seeing something in its particularity, as Rilke describes it, unfolds in the very meandering of his syntax. It proceeds, once he has claimed, "*Das Anschauen ist eine so wunderbare Sache*" (gazing is such a wonderful thing) to circumscribe this wonderful thing that gazing is as an almost incomprehensible confabulation between "object outside" and "event within us":

> Gazing is such a wonderful thing of which we still know so little; with it we are turned completely outward but just when we are most so, things seem to be going on in us that have waited longingly to be unobserved, and while they, untouched and curiously anonymous achieve themselves in us *without us*,—their meaning is growing up in the object outside, a name convincing, strong, the only one possible for them in which we blissfully and reverently recognize the event within us, though we ourselves do not quite reach to it, only quite faintly, quite from afar, comprehending it under the sign of some thing, strange a moment ago and already [the] next moment newly estranged.[4]

Although admittedly somewhat mystifying in its dense complexity, Rilke's main observation seems to amount to the claim—echoing Kant's Transcendental Aesthetic—that in the aesthetic experience there will be a sudden harmony, "a brief moment of symmetry,"[5] between subject and object. And yet, as the imagination aligns itself with the object, the latter nonetheless never becomes an object of desire or knowledge.

The initial, "completely," i.e. self-forgetful, turn to the external world initiates a corresponding internal process that had mysteriously waited to remain "unobserved" but paradoxically "longingly" so, as if the unobserved things within us had been either repressed or secretly desired to be objectified. The unveiling of these "curiously anonymous" internal "things" now happens "*ohne uns*," without our intention or will, externally, felicitously, miraculously, as if in a prelapsarian naming—ostensibly a Romantic idealization of poetry—and which felicity or miracle in turn again repeats itself and is appropriately acknowledged, internally, even as we "do not quite" comprehend this reciprocity or harmony and remain mystified, but "blissfully" so.

The gaze of nature

If Romantic lyrics are compositions of lingering, then Elizabeth Bishop's poetry—Neo-Romantic in its own way—is a composition of the lingering gaze. In her poem "The Moose," the gaze of nature that awakens dreams and pulls the poet after its dream appears angelically in the unlikely form of a "grand, otherworldly" moose that interrupts the journey of a bus. As the moose suddenly materializes from "the impenetrable wood / and stands there, looms, rather / in the middle of the road" and takes her time looking the bus over, the passengers find themselves enchanted by an aura that Benjamin thinks of as the wellspring of poetry and that likely, in Bishop's tranquil recollection, engendered "The Moose": "Why, why do we feel / (we all feel) this sweet / sensation of joy?"[6] The question, justly rhetorical, echoes Rilke's observation in the letter quoted above that we "blissfully and reverently recognize the event within us, though we ourselves do not quite reach to it." The moose's appearance, in other words, briefly corresponds to a complex internal state that had "waited longingly to be unobserved" and is now strangely actualized—soon to be "newly estranged" once the bus continues its journey.

"The Moose," like Rilke's passage from his letter, is structured by an inside–outside binary. Inside is the spatialized clock-time the bus traverses on its scheduled journey. Outside is "the impenetrable wood;" outside is the erasure or stopping of clock-time in the moment of the animal's emergence. What becomes visible in this clashing or overlapping of two temporalities is the paradox of their length, a paradox that we encounter repeatedly in our own lives. The two sides of the paradox are visible 1.) in the 28 lightly rhymed sestets that perform the measurable length of the bus's journey, and 2.) in the brevity of the moose's visitation, where the 33 lines of the moose's appearance within the entirety of the poem feel nonetheless temporally vastly longer than the 141 (strictly counting) of the bus's journey. The structure of this coming together of two temporalities exemplifies the rarity of the occurrence of untimeliness within time, the subversive nature of untimeliness, and the inapplicability of measurement to the latter. My choice of the word "visitation" to mark the moose's appearance implies, moreover, the otherworldliness of such an experience that elicits "this sweet / sensation of joy"; it is an otherworldliness alluded to in Rilke's notion of strangeness "a moment ago" and the "already" that announces a new estrangement. Like the moose, poems are untimely. They interrupt our scheduled journeys. They record and perform visitations; they are outwardly merely brief; they are strange and ever newly estranging. They invite us into moments, brief and at the same time as immeasurably long as the moose's visitation. The supernatural reverberations and the brevity of such a visitation are memorably described by Proust, who suggests that "some explorer of the invisible" conveys them to us "from that divine world to which he has access, to shine for a few moments above ours."[7]

If aesthetic experience, as Adorno (like Rilke) postulates, becomes living experience only by the return of the gaze of its object, then such a reciprocity seems implied in the animal's looking and lingering while simultaneously maintaining a delightful strangeness that we also witness, for example, in "At the Fishhouses," where a seal appears repeatedly: "He stood up in the water and regarded me / steadily, moving his head a little."[8] Neither the moose nor the seal proffer, of course, any excuse or explanation for their respective appearances. Neither visitation can be grasped in a concept or a meaning; both external events metamorphose into what Rilke enigmatically locates "under the sign of some thing" within us that "we ourselves do not quite reach" and that we only "quite faintingly, quite from afar," fleetingly comprehend, "strange a moment ago and already [the] next moment newly estranged." We will witness the evanescence of such moments particularly in Proust and Sebald.

Both "The Moose" and "At the Fishhouses" are narrative poems whose temporality proceeds through attention to the visual particulars, punctuating the linearity of the narrative. In each of Bishop's minute observations, the Sabbath gaze rescues from the obliterating flux of time the singularity of each detail that returns our gaze, so to speak, or renders our gaze vigilant and explicit in the particularity of its description. So, for example, as the bus starts on its journey, the fog's

> ... cold, round crystals
> form and slide and settle
> in the white hens' feathers,
> in gray glazed cabbages,
> on the cabbage roses
> and lupines like apostles....[9]

In their unpunctuated alignment, the verbs "form and slide and settle," articulate and perform the slowness and adjustment of the lingering gaze; in the subsequent lines we follow the gliding of the tiny, cold, round crystals into such unlikely destinations as feathers, cabbages, and lupines. Our eyes, gliding downwards line by line, mimic the temporal movement—the moment, but the long moment—of this short stanza. How is this movement to be imagined? How do fog crystals slide? What do lupines look like? Like apostles. Or do the fog crystals *settle* on the lupines like apostles? The slow movement and the gentle impudence of the simile invite us to experience the stanza as an aesthetic event in its own right, an Emersonian moment as it were, a happy beholding, a Sabbath gaze, a visitation. Like Mallarmé, who looks *at* rather than *through* the rain streaked window in his essay-poem "Crisis of Verse," we momentarily look at the words on the page while the same words also function transparently like the window of the bus to let us see the fog crystals' (almost) invisible gliding.

Eyes

As in "The Moose," in "The Fish" Bishop's videographic eye reverently lingers on the unsightly animal's own exquisite version of otherworldliness, and the question that foregrounds itself, the question the poem must answer, is whether Bishop's aesthetic can justify the ethical quandaries the poem raises. How ethical is it, bluntly, to use the suffering of an animal for a poem? Does the poem attend to the agony of the fish opportunistically, indifferently, empathically? Can empathy even be possible if a creature is merely to serve a poet's aesthetic reverie "While his gills were breathing in / the terrible oxygen / —the frightening gills"?[10]

In one of his aphorisms in *Minima Moralia*, Adorno articulates my concerns when he considers the gaze of the mortally wounded animal and concludes that "the stubbornness by which man rejects this animal gaze, repeats itself in cruelties to humans where the perpetrators endlessly repeat the phrase 'only an animal' in order to convince themselves of something that seemed inconceivable even in the suffering animal."[11] How then, can the aesthetic value, the descriptive precision, the stylistic nuance of Bishop's language, refute such indictment?

Like "The Moose," "The Fish" is structured by a narrative temporality. The poem proceeds from the opening announcement, "I caught a tremendous fish / and held him beside the boat…" to the closing line, "And I let the fish go." In between this somewhat tedious frame of a somewhat unconventional tall fish tale, Bishop describes the fish in most intimate detail as the speaker's gaze—throughout strangely labeled as an invasive "stare"—with the alluring patience of strip tease penetrates the body of the fish to fillet the flesh from the bones. The ingenuity of Bishop's style, the length and nuance, even the novelty and beauty, of her description cannot in itself, I think, refute the charge of aesthetic opportunism or moral indifference. Brett C. Millier's comments in her biography of Bishop to all appearance not only turns a blind eye (so to speak) to the suffering animal—"The 'event' in the poem happens less to the fish than to the fisher"—but reads the gesture of letting the fish go as a "covenant with the other battered creature"[12] which invokes, sentimentally, a wholly unearned solidarity with the hooked animal.

My comments so far might elicit our agreement with John Berger's claim that "animals are always the observed. The fact that they can observe us has lost all significance."[13] Berger's indictment of our moral indifference seems exemplified in the following passage, as the poet looks

>   into his eyes
> which were far larger than mine
> but shallower, and yellowed,
> the irises backed and packed
> with tarnished tinfoil
> seen through the lenses
> of old scratched isinglass.
> They shifted a little, but not
> to return my stare.[14]

But what if we were to heed Nietzsche's advice and read this passage "slowly, profoundly, attentively, prudently, with inner thoughts, with the mental doors ajar, with delicate fingers and eyes?" If gazing, as Rilke exclaims, is such a wonderful thing, what is the wonder that it produces in this missed encounter between poet and fish? Or, if lingering is curative, as Bachelard claims, how does it cure the fish's wounds? The answer lies, I think, in a very small detail, easily missed:

Bishop's lines, as I hope to show, quite unexpectedly perform the kind of metamorphosis Rilke attributes to the gaze in which (to repeat part of his sentence again) "we are turned completely outward but just when we are most so, things seem to be going on in us that have waited longingly to be unobserved." As we trace Rilke's observation in the excerpt above, we will initially find Bishop's lines to offer a close, intimate, and moving description of the animal's eyes. Might these same eyes, so beautifully invoked, in turn reflect the poet's gaze that has "waited, longingly to be unobserved?" Is it in the charged, psychologically overdetermined, ugly word "stare" that the poet's gaze has all along been indicted, vulnerable to such observation? Have we not mildly overlooked the word's incongruity, thus perpetuating the poet's repression of her gaze's motivation? Perhaps that same waiting, desiring, fearing gaze renders the gills, solipsistically, "frightening" rather than frightened. Perhaps we always had a hunch the subjective emphasis of the word "frightening" was suspect.

In its only animated gesture, the shifting of its eye, the fish conveys a faint, fleeting sign of life. Its eyes look back, but not at the poet's stare that remains longingly unobserved. In not returning the poet's gaze, the animal's agonized eyes have asserted—with its last modicum of resistance—an autonomous otherness. It is not the poet's stare but the eye of the fish that now has turned the poet's, or perhaps our, gaze Sabbatical—unexpectedly, *ohne uns*, without our intention, by a grace that befalls us. While the poet's gaze labors through the poem's craft and vision to impart a soul that all along, unbeknownst to her, has lived in the animal, it is finally the animal—without, or despite, the poet's labor—that develops the soul of the poet.[15] The animal is not seen as an object but felt as a being in its own right.

If so, this scene (as does the one in "The Moose") presents itself within the narrative temporality of the poem as the untimeliness of a *punctum*. Like the small detail of the *punctum*, as Barthes suggests in *Camera Lucida*, that disrupts, disturbs, and subverts the coded, narrative *studium* of a photograph,[16] the fish's eyes shifting "a little," convey its infinite, unimaginable suffering. It *subverts* Bishop's tall fish tale as much as it *converts* her gaze into the soulful self-reflection implied in the release of the fish. "In the long, contemplative look," Adorno writes, "in which people and things unfold, the urge towards the object is always deflected, reflected. Contemplation without violence, which is the source of all the joy of truth, presupposes that he who contemplates an object does not incorporate (*einverleibt*) it into himself."[17] And she lets the fish go.

Notes

1. Adorno, *Aesthetic Theory*, 175–176.
2. Benjamin, *Illuminations*, 188.
3. Benjamin here echoes a passage by Proust: "… for it is only ever we ourselves, through our belief that things seen have an existence of their own, who can impart to some of them a soul which lives in them, and which they then develop in us." *In the Shadow of Young Girls in Flower*, 114.
4. *Letters of Rainer Maria Rilke: 1892–1910*, trans. Jane Bannard Greene and M.D. Herter Norton (New York: Norton, 1972), 266.
5. Christian Jany, "'*Das Anschauen ist eine so wunderbare Sache, von der wir noch so wenig wissen*': Szenographien des Schauens beim mittleren Rilke," *Zeitschrift für Aesthetik und Allgemeine Kunstwissenschaft* 59.1 (2014): 147.
6. Elizabeth Bishop, *The Complete Poems: 1927–1979* (New York: Noonday, 1992), 173.
7. Proust, *Swann's Way*, 364.
8. Bishop, *The Complete Poems*, 65.
9. Ibid., 170.
10. Ibid., 42.
11. Adorno, *Minima Moralia*, 233.

12 Brett C. Millier, *Elizabeth Bishop: Life and the Memory of It* (Berkeley: U of California P, 1993), 154.
13 Berger, *About Looking*, 16.
14 Bishop, *The Complete Poems*, 42–43.
15 I here paraphrase Proust's passage mentioned in note 3 above.
16 Barthes, *Camera Lucida*, trans. Richard Howard (New York: Hill and Wang, 1981), 27, 43.
17 Adorno, *Minima Moralia*, #54, 111–112; my trans.

8 Virginia Woolf's indescribable pause

~~Plot~~

In his book on walking, Roger Gilbert writes that "the walk poem typically moves *between* the linear, sequential relation to the world of realism and the epiphanic one of romance," and that the epiphanic moments "are experienced as brief pauses or intervals, after which linearity and flux take over once more."[1] If narratives, like walks, are structured by linearity and flux or, as Sartre for example has argued, by waiting,[2] this structure, Gilbert seems to imply, only works if it is complicated or subverted by epiphanic moments. It is by such subversions that walking is distinguished from pacing, running, rushing, or marching. In their brevity and intensity, epiphanic moments resemble lyric poems. Although brief, they pause and elaborate. If there were no such moments in a novel, it would run its course, as Emerson might say, like our Massachusetts clocks (there are such novels and lives), which, I assume, is why Lukács, privileging Bergsonian temporal interiority over official clock-time,[3] claims that the entire action of a novel consists in "nothing other than a struggle against the might of time."[4]

The temporality of the epiphanic moment is explicitly foregrounded in Clarissa Dalloway's "indescribable pause … before Big Ben strikes"—a "moment of June"[5] that will lengthen to some two hundred pages in Woolf's novel. In other words, *Mrs. Dalloway* is less structured by the linear passage of time during that one day in June on which Mrs. Dalloway intends to throw a party, than by the persistent intrusion of lyric moments. Indeed, so numerous and persistent are these intrusions that Woolf's novel ends up inverting the conventional assumption that lyric time is embedded and contextualized by narrative time, as Gilbert implies when he writes that epiphanic moments occur "within the ongoing temporality of the walk."[6] For here it is the opposite; it is narrative time that becomes provisional and contingent;

and it is not lyric but narrative time that intrudes, especially in the form of the inexorable ringing out of hours and half hours from authoritative steeples and towers. *Mrs. Dalloway* thus comes as close as possible to the ideal novel in which, as Woolf proposes in her essay "Modern Fiction," "there would be no plot, no comedy, no tragedy, no love interest or catastrophe in the accepted style."[7] A similar avant-garde aesthetic is already announced by Whitman, who promises that *Leaves of Grass* would not "carry out, in the approved style, some choice plot of fortune or misfortune, or fancy, or fine thoughts, or incidents, or courtesies."[8]

Although there are plenty of fancy fine thoughts, incidents, and a few courtesies in *Mrs. Dalloway,* Woolf's novel still confirms Barthes' claim that we read classical fiction with little concern for "the integrity of the text" but rather with a certain "avidity for knowledge" (which Barthes compares to strip-tease) and which makes us, Barthes thinks, secretly "to skim or to skip[9] (in French literally "overfly" and "overleap") such tedious passages as descriptions, explications, considerations, and conversations. The plot of Woolf's novel by contrast—Mrs. Dalloway's old suitor shows up while she intends to give a party that evening—would hardly reward such haste and impatience. For the outcome of Woolf's *plot*—presumably intentionally boring by conventional standards—is always already known.

What *Mrs. Dalloway* has in common with the other novels I discuss in this book, and with Whitman's "Song of Myself," is that there is nothing to abbreviate or disregard since there is nothing really to know in the way of plot. What is to be known occurs not in the narrative but in the lyrical moments and passages—the inner thoughts and monologues, the memories and reflections, the daydreaming and conjecturing—that the "avid" reader of a realistic novel would regard merely as obstacles to his desire— I gender my language intentionally—for the swift resolution of the plot. No doubt, Eliot's memorable "young man carbuncular" in *The Waste Land* who assaults the typist in eight quick lines on, I imagine, the lily patterned couch of her bedsitter has read neither Whitman nor Woolf.[10]

Untimeliness

Mrs. Dalloway famously opens with Clarissa's "plunge...into the open air. How fresh, how calm," Clarissa exclaims to herself, "like the flap of a wave; the kiss of a wave; chill and sharp."[11] The lyric's brevity and intensity are amplified in the words "fresh," "calm," "pause," "plunge," "flap," "kiss," even as these one-syllable words announce a dense and yet fleeting temporality immeasurable by the insistent striking and slicing of hours in the novel. Although the novel's first sentence tells us that Mrs. Dalloway is merely out and about to buy flowers, the beautiful is a feeling, not a bunch of flowers; a temporal experience, not a material thing.[12] None of the sensory impressions—Clarissa's luxuriating in the air, its freshness, its calm, its kiss, its chill, its sharpness, its likeness to a wave—is solid or materially tangible; all of them are subjective and evanescent; all of them are beautiful, distinct, precise; none of them is a thing one could put on a shelf.

Clarissa's life is a solitary duration as Merleau-Ponty would call it;[13] she embodies and performs the untimeliness that constitutes the human subject in Kant's or in Bergson's aesthetic. *Mrs. Dalloway*, exemplary modernist narrative that it is, is wholly conceived and structured by solitary durations. Susceptible to the visitations of the beautiful, Clarissa serves as a veritable paragon of one who has mastered the art of lingering—though when in the opening pages she "stiffened a little on the kerb, waiting for Durtnall's van to pass," when the paragraph ends with "There she perched ... waiting to cross, very upright,"[14] her stiffening and uprightness tell us that she is here precisely *not* lingering. And yet, Clarissa's waiting to cross Victoria Street "in the midst of the traffic" has none of the fretful restlessness characteristic of waiting as I've described it, for now she moves from the temporality of waiting effortlessly into that of lingering:

> For having lived in Westminster—how many years now? over twenty,—one feels even in the midst of the traffic, or walking at night, Clarissa was positive, a particular hush, or solemnity; an indescribable pause; a suspense (but that might be her heart, affected, they said, by influenza) before Big Ben strikes. There! Out it boomed. First a warning, musical; then the hour, irrevocable. The leaden circles dissolved in the air. Such fools we are, she thought, crossing Victoria Street.[15]

Even the syntax performs Clarissa's lingering in her sentence, suspended as it is in its alternations, interspersions, declarations, and qualifications. Although her lingering is accompanied by Big Ben's musical prelude, the official time in which her waiting will come to an end has nothing musical about it; it is "the hour, irrevocable." *Mrs. Dalloway* proves, however, that the "leaden" hours that Big Ben strikes are irrevocable only to those whose lives are weighed down by them. For leaden hours can be dissolved—as they are in the sinuous unfolding of the novel. Each iteration of lingering numerously and variously performed by the novel's characters revokes the hour irrevocable. For each iteration slows and lengthens, stalls and expands the hours rung from towers and turrets. In *Mrs. Dalloway*, the hours melt like Dali's clocks.

The privileges of idleness

Clarissa's belief that her living in Westminster would have produced a particular hush or solemnity illustrates Benjamin's observation, quoted earlier, that "idleness is marked by features of the capitalist economic order in which it flourishes"[16] and which association echoes the Romantic philosopher Friedrich Schlegel's claim that idleness is a right that distinguishes the aristocracy from the bourgeoisie.[17] Thus, Clarissa's contemplations about her fashionable address, her simultaneous immersion in and detachment from her immediate surroundings, her thought of walking at night, her pondering of her health, all reflect her social and economic privilege. Her ruminations are unsurprisingly generalized or standardized as supposedly occurring not just to her but to any "one" having lived in Westminster. These privileges are on display in the slowness of the sentence as it lingers between and beyond the subject and the predicate and by which slowness the hush, the pause, the solemnity, the suspense syntactically and stylistically—but also economically and morally—come about.

And yet again, these economic and moral dimensions define Clarissa Dalloway as little as do the hours rung out by Big Ben. The fullness of her interior, contemplative life is summed up in Peter Walsh's ecstatic recognition in the novel's last line: "For there she was."[18] For it is Clarissa who, at that moment, is the time that passes; she embodies Rilke's authentic self-completion in *Hiersein*. She has her being, at least momentarily, in an infinite realm of duration. Earlier in the novel she muses,

> She was not old yet. She had just broken into her fifty-second year. Months and months of it were still untouched. June, July, August! Each still remained almost whole, and, as if to catch the falling drop, Clarissa (crossing to the dressing table) plunged into the very heart of the moment, transfixed it, there—the moment of this June morning....[19]

The inversion of time and duration, of narrative and lyric time is here represented *en miniature*. Clarissa's inner life dominates the brief narrative of this paragraph to such an extent that the visible, external action—"(crossing to the dressing table)"—needs to be mentioned only in parentheses. Compared to the temporality of "the moment of this

June morning," the spatial crossing of the room, and the materiality of the dressing table, appear banal and merely circumstantial. While the paragraph exemplifies the modernist novel's focus on duration rather than spatial linearity, this duration only emerges as Clarissa abandons her initial fixation on measurable time, the years and months of her life, and yields to "the very heart of the moment."

Paul Ricoeur interprets the moment into which Clarissa plunges in this passage as representing "her love of life, of perishable beauty, of changing light," and as "her passion for 'the falling drop.'"[20] Although externally Clarissa inhabits this lyrical interlude only as a temporary reprieve from the irrevocable hour; inwardly, in her solitary duration, the catching of the falling drop appoints the "heart of the moment"; the falling drop outlasts the measurable hour and all the hours struck by Big Ben and all the subsidiary clocks. Even more than her love of life, or her love of perishable beauty, or her love of changing light, it is her passion for "the falling drop" that embodies the sudden intensity of Carissa's insight into the duration of her life. The "falling drop" is a metaphor for *Mrs. Dalloway* the novel and Mrs. Dalloway the character. We witness its falling in our reading of the novel at the end of which Clarissa poignantly sums up her life as a mere temporality: "Nothing could be slow enough; nothing last too long."[21] No falling drop could fall slowly enough, no falling drop last too long. The hour doesn't measure up to it.

The economics of idleness

It is in Hugh Whitebread that the economic and moral qualities by which idleness is complicit with the capitalist economic order are sardonically indicted. The old man splendidly acts his part as he gazes at "a commercial clock, suspended above a shop in Oxford Street": "(so Hugh Whitebread ruminated, dallying there in front of the shop window.)" His idleness—focused on the time that is money by contrast to Clarissa's focus on "the very heart of the moment"—appears in parentheses as if to indict the privilege of its seclusion while he pays his respect to authoritative clocks that "naturally took the form later of buying off Rigby and Lowndes socks or shoes."[22] Woolf's irony is hardly subtle when Mr. Whitebread considers the issue of "stamp[ing] out immorality in parks" while he cuts "[a] magnificent figure ... pausing for a moment (as the sound of the half hour died away) to look critically, magisterially, at socks and shoes."[23] If Mr. Whitebread's frivolous dallying were not wholly commensurate with the privilege time and money afford, it would be merely amusing or pitiable.

If we are left to wonder whether lingering is a temporality reserved for the rich, whether the poor wait while the rich enjoy the thought of buying shoes or socks at Rigby and Lowndes, we find the poor, early in the novel, waiting in front of Buckingham Palace to catch a glimpse of royalty: "poor women waiting to see the Queen go past—poor women, nice little children, orphans, widows."[24] The erasure of the individual in the presentation of their lives as an anonymous collective forces the poor into an idleness, as Rousseau observes, " 'that is deadly because it is obligatory' " while " 'the idleness of solitude is delightful because it is free and voluntary.' "[25] Contemplative lingering, in other words, is a temporality reserved for the individual just as the beautiful is visible only in the singular. The poor, whose immorality in the parks needs stamping out, are plural.

The obligatory idleness of the poor is in plain view for Richard Dalloway, who wanders, flowers in hand, through Green Park, "observing with pleasure how in the shade of the trees whole families, poor families, were sprawling; children kicking up their legs; sucking milk; paper bags thrown about" and in which observation his benevolently patronizing gaze merrily jumbles together families, children, milk, and paper bags. His subsequent musings, "But what could be done for female vagrants," imply that collecting paper bags and keeping the parks open in the summer might just be what could be done for poor families. One particular "female vagrant," emanating a faint exoticism as Mr. Dalloway considers the problem, seems more appealing:

> But what could be done for female vagrants like that poor creature, stretched on her elbow (as if she had flung herself on the earth, rid of all ties, to observe curiously, to speculate boldly, to consider the whys and wherefores, impudent, loose-lipped, humorous), he did not know.[26]

Evidently, "that poor creature" cannot emerge as anything other than a particular specimen of a certain interesting poverty. In her generic anonymity, barred from subjectivity and contemplation, she mutely suffers Richard Dalloway's condescending projections—all in his head—especially his bold speculations about "the whys and wherefores" that elicit his immediate judgement—as if *she* had entertained *his* misgivings—of the cheeky impudence, confirmed in the attribution of loose lips, and finally made light of in the humor that forgives the insolence of a woman's vain speculations.

Inconclusive and more than slightly creepy as these musings and projections remain, the question about female vagrancy occurs to

Mr. Dalloway tantalizingly yet again as he (flowers in hand) approaches her, passes her, while "she laughed at the sight of him," while "he smiled good-humouredly." His wandering thought—all the while elaborated by the slow deliberateness of the passage—that "still there was time for a spark between them" moves into yet a murkier light his repeated consideration of "the problem of the female vagrant," so that it turns out necessary, as he by now has thankfully passed the object of his brief infatuation, finally to abandon this scene of erotic fantasy: "not that they would ever speak," and which elicits his sheepish, wholly inauthentic resolve seamlessly added to his ruminations "to tell Clarissa that he loved her, in so many words."[27]

Since the nameless woman—on whom Richard Dalloway has lavished more thoughts than he will have words for Clarissa—languidly "stretched on her elbow" like a bather at the beach, morbid and erotic at once, has "flung herself on the earth," she foreshadows the suicide of the war-traumatized Septimus Smith who, we read further on, "flung himself vigorously, violently down on to Mrs. Filmer's area railings."[28] The woman, too, as if to make that association yet more explicit, is "rid of all ties," and the question remains open whether poverty might make one fling oneself on the earth much less vigorously and violently than a suicide.

What emerges, then, from these considerations is that devoid of articulation or interiority the woman's lingering amounts to an endurance of time's wholly anonymous, accidental incarnation in some human specimen in some urban park where lingering is *de rigeur*; it exemplifies Rousseau's notion of involuntary lingering imposed on the poor; it is the mute material endurance of body and mind without recourse to any other expression than the illicit curiosity and speculation projected onto her by the Mr. Dalloways of the world. Here duration sounds no Bergsonian melody; it is merely a cacophonous din.

The lingering of writing

Shortly before the front-doorbell rings and Peter Walsh breaks into the eternal Sunday into which Clarissa Dalloway is born, we find her mending a tear in the fabric of her dress.

> Quiet descended on her, calm, content, as her needle, drawing the silk smoothly to its gentle pause, collected the green folds together and attached them, very lightly, to the belt.[29]

Suspending its indirect object to the very end, slowing its flow by no fewer than seven commas, the sentence performs in its tense and syntax the temporality of Clarissa's lingering. (If my reader were perchance to find herself to count the commas, she would have briefly reverted to the unmusical dimension of time instead of the musical dimension of duration.) The needle functions as a metaphoric pen, drawing the folds of the texture of the sentence; it draws "the green folds" of the silk "smoothly to its gentle pause" at the end of the sentence. The sentence lingers; it performs and comments at once on the pause reached at the end. Like the silk that Clarissa attaches "very lightly" to the belt, Woolf's pen "very lightly" attaches itself to the end of the sentence and thus writes out, sews up, mends—as if a tear in time, fills and completes it; makes it into a moment. Clarissa's quiet, calm contentment appears in the rhythm and syntax of the sentence; the rhythm and syntax work like a repair for the tear—they allegorize Woolf's writing and the project of her novel of which the evening dress for the party—like Laertes' shroud in *The Odyssey*–is a metaphor.

The paragraph continues by adding to the significance of this rhythm a cosmic analogy that underscores the therapeutic properties of the temporality within which Clarissa performs her sewing, and that we mentioned with reference to Bachelard, and within which Woolf, like Penelope at her loom, weaves her writing:

> So on a summer's day waves collect, overbalance, and fall; collect and fall; and the whole world seems to be saying "that is all" more and more ponderously, until even the heart in the body which lies in the sun on the beach says too, That is all. Fear no more, says the heart. Fear no more, says the heart, committing its burden to some sea, which sighs collectively for all sorrows, and renews, begins, collects, lets fall.[30]

It is as if Woolf were writing these waves with a weaver's shuttle to accompany the sighs of the sea, passing her thread from weft to warp—"renews, begins, collects, lets fall"—as if she were sewing water. The scene is a transcription of the temporality of lingering; it is self-sufficient, complete, rhythmic, cosmic, an *ars poetica* of Woolf's style, a performative of Kristeva's sensuous semiotic, an articulation of Bergson's melody of duration. Although the scene is set on a summer's day, it is reminiscent of Woolf's short essay entitled "The Moment: Summer's Night," where she argues that the moment, while "composed of visual and of sense impressions," is a temporality wherein one "seeks out the different elements ... in order to compose the truth of it, the whole of it."[31] The moment—vague, indeterminate, immeasurable in length—in which one lingers, daydreams, loafs, or whiles away one's time is a matter of *com-position*—etymologically a putting-together, a sewing and mending. The moment re-members; while clock-time dis-members; "the day," Benjamin writes, "unravels what the night was woven."[32] Woolf's writing is a nocturnal weaving, a composition of moments.

Chronotopes

Moments are whole. They do not have the ragged edges of waiting. They are, as Woolf's word "to compose" implies, the temporal site of artistic expression, of poems or paintings especially. In Proust, such moments as we will see, often assume the musical form of a composition. Similar to Bachelard, Georges Poulet thinks of the moment spatially *"comme un lieu de la durée,"* as a site of duration.[33] Woolf's sentence—if we imagine it, for example, in brief syllabic lineation—could be transcribed into such a site that would highlight its compositional, spatial wholeness. "[A] poet can shape time in a poem," Glyn Maxwell suggests, "and form is how that's done."[34]

> Quiet descended on her,
> calm, content,
> as her needle,
> drawing the silk
> smoothly
> to its gentle pause,
> collected the green
> folds together and
> attached them,
> very lightly,
> to the belt.

The quiet that descends on Clarissa Dalloway is as existential as it is aesthetic; it defines her being; it is her solitary duration; it is who she is. The sentence whose auditory resonance I have tried to make visible in the lineation above is the site of a human identity.

If lyric poems are composed in the temporality of lingering, they are sites of humanity. They are stanzas, rooms, furnished not with chairs and tables but with lines and words. Or to say the same slightly differently, "poems are constructed models of time" as Susan Stewart writes.[35] They are sites of (our) duration where (our) duration briefly transforms to space, where time is briefly visible as it lingers in the words on the page, as it makes the words turn and pass and turn slowly, "renews, begins, collects, lets fall,"—the punctuation and line breaks orchestrating the rhythm—from line to line, from weft to warp, like the long, slow, quiet breath of a sleeper. Poems, in other words, are spaces of time, like theatre, chronotopes,[36] implied in the word *stanza* (room) where we have our being. Such is the case memorably in Emily Dickinson's stanza,

> I dwell in Possibility—
> A fairer House than Prose—
> More numerous of Windows—
> Superior—for Doors—[37]

The poem is a metaphysical conceit. Possibility—Aristotle's word for poetry—here becomes the poet's dwelling place. One dwells in a poem; one makes it one's room; one doesn't pass through it. In Aristotle's *Poetics*, the historian "describes the thing that has been," while the poet "the thing that might be."[38] The distinction is between temporalities; one is closed and past, the other is open and ongoing. But slowly, for in the present of possibility, the future is suspended.

We encounter such a space, explicitly contextualized but at the same time excerpted from the bustle of the city, toward the end of *Mrs. Dalloway*:

> And in the large square where the cabs shot and swerved so quick, there were loitering couples, dallying, embracing, shrunk up under the shower of a tree; that was moving; so silent, so absorbed, that one passed, discretely, timidly, as if in the presence of some sacred ceremony to interrupt which would have been impious.[39]

Moments are whole. Sequestered in a lyrical interlude, the couples' embrace embodies the ceremony of poetry, "so silent, so absorbed" that the passer-by only witnesses, shyly, its hermetic, untimely quality, which is the solitude of lovers whose dallying, slowed and lengthened by eleven punctuation marks, "under the shower of a tree," makes a room for them. The room is the stanza framed by the tree; the couples perform the writing on the page, so that this passage too invites its transcription—to delay and expand its duration—into the silent, absorbed lineation of a poem. I have broken the lines where the syntax would normally accelerate in order to slow the tempo of this sentence, to highlight the temporality of Woolf's prose as it performs "the essential speech of detour," to use Blanchot's terms, "the 'poetry' in the turn of writing ... wherein time turns, saying time as turning."[40]

> And in the large square
> where the cabs
> shot and swerved so
> quick, there
> were loitering
> couples, dallying,
> embracing, shrunk up under
> the shower of a tree; that
> was moving; so
> silent, so
> absorbed, that
> one passed,
> discretely, timidly, as if
> in the presence of some
> sacred ceremony
> to interrupt which
> would have been impious.

The sentence lingers in the pauses before the repeated relative pronoun "that," which denotes the lovers' inviolate space within which the tree's movement emits its intimate and solemn aura; the tree's movement, slightly paused in the ungrammatical semicolon, thereafter lingers in the conjunctions "so" and "as if" emphasizing, qualifying each adjective; it lingers finally in the unusual placement of the relative pronoun "which." Time in the arrangement of these words passes gently, almost inaudibly, almost sleepily. Woolf's passage—it is both a passage of writing and of time—conjoins a space with time, makes time visible as space, as does the stanza of the poem. A stanza is a space that is time.

In his essay "Field," Berger reports that on his way home from work, he was often obliged to wait for a "minute or two" in front of a railway crossing, and that during this time, "It is as though these minutes fill a certain area of time which exactly fits the spatial area of the field. Time and space conjoin."[41] In sleep, even more than in lingering, time and space conjoin most intensely. The person who lingers is already on her way to bed. "My person is not simply situated where I sleep," Blanchot writes, "it is this very site, and my sleeping is the fact that now my abode is my being."[42]

Time as a garden

In her comments about her writing—deeply indebted to Woolf's novels—Jeanette Winterson's work gradually assumes the dimensions of a poetic dwelling place.

My work is rooted in silence. It grows out of deep beds of contemplation, where words, which are living things, can form and re-form into new wholes. What is visible, the finished books, are underpinned by the fertility of uncounted hours. A writer has no use for the clock. A writer lives in an infinity of days, time without end, ploughed under.[43]

The paragraph's conceit of writing as a garden imagines a garden as a temporality. A passionate gardener, Winterson attunes her work to the slowness of plant growth. Rooted in silence, it grows out of deep beds of contemplation; like plants, words become living things, forming and reforming until the blooming of the book.[44] What feeds this slow growth of a book are the uncounted hours, spent in a time without end, invisibly "ploughed under" the covers of the book— even as the metaphor "ploughed under" also implies the death of the author, as it were, between the covers of her book. There is only one thing to show for this accounting of the infinitely slow creative process: the book, the deceptively material book, that is. As an object, the book conceals the invisible hours just as the clock would measure them in vain. The creative process unfolds, like Bergson's *durée*, invisibly, immeasurably, almost indescribably. Its beginnings rest in silence; contemplation lies unseen in "deep beds"; and words, like Bergson's time, move, change, evolve as they are written. The writer's work remains unaccounted for, anonymous, almost betrayed by the object of the book.

But only almost. The book is finally to be understood not as an object but as repository of the writer's "infinity of days." Once the book is opened, the reader stoops over the book as the gardener stoops over her bed of seeds. The reader's silence echoes the writer's silence; his solitude extends her solitude, an infinitely slow process of growth commences, of words as "living things," forming and re-forming in the reader into new wholes. Let us call the book a time. Let us call time a book. Let us open the book and time will have no end. A reader has no use for the clock.

Notes

1 Gilbert, *Walks in the World*, 17–18.
2 Cf. Mark Currie, "Reading in Time" in Allen, 40.
3 Cf. Charles M. Tung, "Technology and Time: Clocks, Time Machines, and Speculation" in Allen, 169.
4 Lukács, *Die Theorie des Romans*, 109; cf. Berger, *About Looking*, 204.
5 Virginia Woolf, *Mrs. Dalloway* (New York: Harcourt Brace & Co., 1981), 4.

6 Gilbert, *Walks in the World*, 18.
7 Virginia Woolf, *The Common Reader*, ed. Andrew McNeillie (New York: Harcourt Brace Jovanovich, 1984), 150.
8 Whitman, "A Backward Glance o'er Travel'd Roads" in *Complete Poetry and Collected Prose*, 662.
9 Barthes, *The Pleasure of the Text*, 11; in the original French the passage reads: "*l'avidité même de la connaissance nous entraîne à survoler ou à enjamber certains passages (pressentis 'ennuyeux')* ... *nous sautons impunément (personne nous ne voit) les descriptions, les explications, les considérations, les conversations.*" *Le Plaisir du texte* (Paris: Éditions du Seuil, 1973), 21.
10 Eliot, *The Complete Poems and Plays*, 68.
11 Woolf, *Mrs. Dalloway*, 4, 3.
12 Cf. Adorno, *Aesthetic Theory*, 164.
13 Merleau-Ponty, *Signs*, 186.
14 Woolf, *Mrs. Dalloway*, 4.
15 Ibid.
16 Benjamin, *The Arcades Project*, 805.
17 Schlegel, "Idylle über den Müßiggang" in *Kritische Friedrich-Schlegel-Ausgabe*, 26: "*ist es das Recht des Müssiggangs was Vornehme und Gemeine unterscheidet, und das eigentliche Prinzip des Adels.*"
18 Woolf, *Mrs. Dalloway*, 194.
19 Ibid., 36–37.
20 Paul Ricoeur, *Time and Narrative*, trans. Kathleen Blamey and David Pellauer, vol. 2 (Chigago, U of Chicago P., 1985), 110.
21 Woolf, *Mrs. Dalloway*, 185.
22 Ibid., 102.
23 Ibid., 103.
24 Ibid., 20.
25 Quoted in Benjamin, *The Arcades Project*, 805.
26 Woolf, *Mrs. Dalloway*, 116.
27 Ibid.
28 Ibid., 149.
29 Ibid., 39.
30 Ibid., 39–40.
31 Virginia Woolf, "The Moment: Summer's Night" in *Collected Essays*, vol. 2 (New York: Harcourt Brace & World, Inc. 1967), 293.
32 Benjamin, *Illuminations*, 202.
33 Georges Poulet, *Études sur le temps humain*, vol. 3 (Paris: Librairie Plon, 1964), 16.
34 Glyn Maxwell, *On Poetry* (Cambridge: Harvard UP, 2013), 29.
35 Stewart, *Poetry and the Fate of the Senses*, 227.
36 Matthew Wagner, "Time and Theatre," in Allen, 67.
37 Emily Dickinson, *The Complete Poems* (London: Faber and Faber, 1986), #657.
38 Aristotle, *Rhetoric and Poetics*, trans. W. Rhys Roberts and Ingram Bywater (New York: Modern Library, 1954), 243–35.
39 Woolf, *Mrs. Dalloway*, 163.
40 Blanchot, *The Infinite Conversation*, 23.
41 Berger, *About Looking*, 200.

42 Maurice Blanchot, *The Space of Literature*, trans. Ann Smock (Lincoln: U of Nebraska P, 1982), 266.
43 Winterson, *Art Objects*, 169.
44 Cf. Whitman, "A Backward Glance o'er Travel'd Roads" in *Complete Poetry and Collected Prose*, where he conceives the preparation for *Leaves of Grass* as "my poetic field, with the particular and general plowing, planting, seeding, and occupation of the ground, till everything fertilized, rooted, and ready to start its own way for good or bad" (664).

9 Proustian interludes

The everyday hour

"What was it that Proust sought so frenetically?" Walter Benjamin asks in his essay "The Image of Proust":

> What was at the bottom of these infinite efforts? Can we say that all lives, works, and deeds that matter were never anything but the undisturbed unfolding of the most banal, most fleeting, most sentimental, weakest hour in the life of the one to whom they pertain? When Proust in a well-known passage described the hour that was most his own, he did it in such a way that everyone can find it in his own existence. We might almost call it an everyday hour; it comes with the night, [in] a lost twittering [...] or a breath drawn at the sill of an open window.[1]

The hour's undisturbed unfolding (*unbeirrte Entfaltung*) comes almost casually, impartially, indifferently, certainly unexpectedly "with the night, in a lost twittering, or in the breath drawn at the open window"—if only, Benjamin cautions, "we were less inclined to give in to sleep." While we, alas, are ever so inclined, "Proust," Benjamin adds, "did not give in to sleep."[2] Thus, "in the hour that was most his own," in the banal, fleeting, sentimental, weak, childish twilight hours of Proust's nocturnal lingering in a cork-lined room on Boulevard Haussmann in Paris over the taste of a mere *madeleine*, for example, we might find the origin of his infinite efforts.

In our lives, everyday hours are usually underestimated, even neglected, and forgotten; we waste them either to go to sleep or to earn a hundred dollars. Were it not so, I, too, might be a famous novelist. For Benjamin, everyday hours arrive as sequestered, intimate, unexpected moments whose unspectacular coming and passing we easily miss: a lost twittering; a breath drawn at the sill of an open window; the moment when the sun silvers the tips of the high grass, the moment when the wind makes the meadow move like water; the sounds of the house at night. But these are the moments that matter; they bring about the lives, and works, and deeds that matter.

I assume the "well-known" passage to which Benjamin alludes is the one early in *Swann's Way* that occurs—significantly—one inconspicuous "day in winter, as I returned home," a "gloomy" day foreshadowing "another sad day to follow." It is an ordinary day on which Marcel's mother, noticing her child is cold, offers him "a little tea," and "one of those squat plump cakes called *petites madeleines*." The event so far bears all the characteristics of Benjamin's common "everyday hour." The only unusual occurrence on this otherwise unremarkable day is that little Marcel—whose name I invoke as a form of fictional self-invention[3]—takes his tea "*contre mon habitude*," against my habit, which provides a small aperture in the ordinary to let in the extraordinary that will turn, astonishingly, into thousands of pages of writing in seven volumes of *A la recherche du temps perdu*:

> But at the very instant when the mouthful of tea mixed with cake crumbs touched my palate, I quivered, attentive to the extraordinary thing that was happening inside me. A delicious pleasure had invaded me, isolated me, without my having any notion as to its cause. It had immediately rendered the vicissitudes of life unimportant to me, its disasters innocuous, its brevity illusory, acting in the same way that love acts, by filling me with a precious essence: or rather this essence was not merely inside me, it was me.[4]

A writer, as we recall Winterson's phrase, has no use for the clock. How similar this passage is to Emerson's journal entry reporting on his walk from Boston to Cambridge about finding a sunny spot far from Massachusetts clocks, how similar to Nietzsche's paragraph about the ecstasies of slow reading, how similar to Coleridge's sudden delight under the lime-tree bower, how similar to Clarissa Dalloway's indescribable pause. It is at this moment—literalizing in Marcel's *tasting* of the *madeleine* Kant's metaphor of *taste* and bearing all the features of accident and trespass of the Kantian aesthetic experience—when the novel's temporality changes from *mémoire volontaire* to *mémoire involontaire*, from waiting—for mama to put Marcel to bed—to the endless lingering that will be Proust's sleepless work. While this moment occurs well into the first chapter of *Swann's Way*, it presents itself as the beginning of the book. It is a moment that is the essence of Proust as it is the essence of his writing, a solitary fortuity.

Although we might want to believe that *A la recherche du temps perdu* is the work of Proust's heroically decadent "remembering, waiting, hoping, upon all the ruins of the rest,"[5] his novel originates neither in remembering, nor in waiting, nor in hoping, nor in the flippantly proffered ruins of the rest. Rather, it originates in the hour that was most his own, the hour opened "*contre mon habitude,*" the accidental, surprising, unanticipated hour, "through which we can retrieve any part of us," as Proust explains in *In the Shadow of Young Girls in Flower*; "that the reasoning mind, having no use for it, disdained, the last vestige of the past, the best of it, the part which, after all our tears seem to have dried, can make us weep again."[6]

In his commentary on Kafka, Blanchot describes this transformation from the past to the present, from design to accident, from memory to weeping, from a measurable to an immeasurable temporality. Writing a novel, Blanchot declares in his inimitable vintage of chiasmus and paradox,

> ... is not a matter of devoting time to the task, of passing one's time writing, but of passing into another time where there is no longer any task; it is a matter of approaching that point where time is lost, where one enters into the fascination and the solitude of time's absence.[7]

In light—or twilight, as we shall see—of Blanchot's paragraph, we might understand Proust's writing *In Search of Lost Time* as a writing in search of the loss of time, of time's absence, or to say the same, as a writing in search of that—disdained by the reasoning mind—which can make us weep again. In other words, while voluntary memory consciously attempts to *remember* a time that is no longer present, involuntary memory is unconsciously present without the conscious act of remembering. Now the absence of time is in the presence of writing. Now the writing proceeds from an author who determines, as Barthes explains quaintly, "to be like the *madeleine* that slowly dissolves in the mouth, which at that moment, is idle. The subject allows himself to disintegrate through memory, and he is idle. If he were not idle, he would find himself once more in the domain of voluntary memory."[8] While such idleness, we might say, constitutes a slow and somewhat alarming self-cannibalistic variation of the death of the author, Barthes' point is clearly that Proust needs to be read slowly, like a *madeleine* that dissolves in the mouth. Proust's observation in the paragraph above about the origin of his pleasure, "without my having any notion as to its cause," refers, of course, to the pleasure of the taste of the *madeleine*; but that sensuous pleasure in turn causes the pleasure of writing that is experienced as mere idleness. And it is likewise with such idleness, Barthes suggests, that one reads Proust: "Proust is what comes to me, not what I summon up."[9] Proust comes to us like sleep.

Sleep / waking

Like Kant's aesthetic, like poetry, like lingering, "sleep is disinterestedness," Blanchot writes in his brief, illuminating essay entitled "Sleep, Night."[10] In sleep one withdraws, he claims, not only from everything but even from oneself. All the attributes that Blanchot assigns to sleep where "I retire from the world's immensity and its disquietude"[11] are attributes of lingering. One lingers by retiring from the world's fierce solicitations, but one must linger, as Blanchot advises, with *sangfroid*,[12] which is to say, it takes a certain courage or daring to linger when the world expects us to hustle. It takes guts to stroll or to loaf when the world wants us to march or to run. Whitman, to all accounts, is likely our most intrepid sleep loafer. "To sleep with open eyes," Blanchot goes on, "is an anomaly symbolically indicating something which the general consciousness does not approve of."[13]

Shortly after Marcel's transformative experience with the taste of the *madeleine*, the tense, significantly, shifting from the past to the present, Proust recounts his strenuous efforts to repeat—

> ... this unknown state which brought with it no logical proof, but only the evidence of its felicity, its reality, and in whose presence the other states of consciousness faded away. I want to try to make it reappear. I return in my thoughts to the moment when I took the first spoonful of tea. I find the same state again, without any new clarity. I ask my mind to make another effort, to bring back once more the sensation that is slipping away. And, so that nothing may interrupt the thrust with which it will try to grasp it again, I clear away every obstacle, every foreign idea, I protect my ears and my attention from the noises in the next room.[14]

Proust's attempts to tap once more into his *mémoire involontaire* resemble the attempts of someone trying to fall asleep. It is a paraphrase of Keats's "Sonnet to Sleep" where sleep, as in Proust's passage, obstinately refuses to come. It is the *trying* that keeps it from coming. Like sleep, Proust's *mémoire involontaire* arrived without cause or logical proof and in whose presence other states of consciousness faded away. But like sleep, his *mémoire involontaire* cannot be called up, ordered, grasped: I want to go to sleep. I find the same state again. I ask my mind to make another effort. I will try to grasp it again. I protect my ears from the noises in the next room. But sleep, like *mémoire involontaire* comes with no logical proof; it is gently to displace other states of consciousness. Proust's most famous predecessor in this displacement of consciousness is Dante, who enters his *Inferno* "full of sleep,"[15] and without whose sleep we would have no *Divina Commedia*.

Good sleep produces lingering, all night long. Bad sleep produces waiting—all night long, from minute to minute, from hour to hour. Good sleep happens in the melody of duration, in the humming of life's depths; bad sleep happens in dreadfully measurable clock-time. The person who sleeps well *lingers* in her sleep, whereas the bad sleeper *waits* for the morning; she resembles the impatient waiter who, according to Blanchot, "tosses and turns in search of that genuine place."[16] Like a bad sleeper, Marcel resolves,

> Ten times I must begin again, lean down toward it. And each time, the laziness that deters us from every difficult task, every work of importance, has counseled me to leave it, to drink my tea and think only about my worries of today, my desires for tomorrow, upon which I may ruminate effortlessly.[17]

It is easier to drink tea than to fall asleep. Hedged about by worries of today and desires of tomorrow, the writer must take his counsel from the sleeper, not from the insomniac who waits on worries and desires, nor from the busy burner of the candle's two ends who will herself burn out. For, when "suddenly the memory appeared"[18] for Marcel, it appears precisely when he has given up on grasping it. Sleep is what comes to me, not what I summon up.

Since sleep is already implied in daydreaming or reverie or stopping by woods on snowy evenings, the temporality of sleep is an extension, an intensification, indeed a clarification of the untimely temporality of lingering. It is no accident that sleep is such a central trope, especially in *Swann's Way*, which begins with the famous line "For a long time, I went to bed early." A bit further on we read that "A sleeping man holds in a circle around him the sequence of the hours, the order of the years and worlds. He consults them instinctively as he wakes,"[19] which identifies the author of *A la recherche du temps perdu* perhaps not quite as a sleeping man but as a man whose writing comes about in a twilight, as that between sleeping and waking. In French, this liminal temporal zone is slightly emphasized in the gerund "*en s'éveillant*," which translates into "while he was waking." Proust, we might say, wrote his work while he was waking. He wrote not giving in to sleep, as Benjamin tells us, yet he drew out of sleep what one would not remember in waking.

It is in the third volume of *In Search of Lost Time*, *The Guermantes Way*, where Proust elaborates on how this gerund form of awakening, *en s'éveillant*, illustrates the complex liminality of involuntary memory:

> The great modification brought about by awakening is not so much our entry into the clear life of consciousness as the loss of all memory of the slightly more subdued light in which our mind had been resting, as in the opaline depths of the sea. The half-veiled thoughts on which we were still drifting a moment ago involved us in quite enough motion for us to refer to them as wakefulness. But, then, our awakenings themselves involve an interruption of memory. A short time later, we describe what preceded them as sleep because we no longer remember it.[20]

Since it is in sleep's "subdued light," "in the opaline depths of the sea," in "half-veiled thoughts" where involuntary memory is spawned, one should by all means stay asleep, for awakening only brings about a loss of memory. But if Prufrock had been merely a pair of ragged claws scuttling across the floors of silent seas, we would have no poem. Neither do "the opaline depths of the sea" nor does "the clear life of consciousness" on its own produce a novel. Proust's art of writing is, instead, to prolong the liminal state between sleep and waking. His work is not to give in to sleep. His work is not to awaken. The suspension or prolongation of this liminality is what we do when we linger. We linger but slightly outside the perimeters of sleep. When we linger, we are as if asleep in a time of which, when we awaken, we can hardly speak other than as poets.

The music of time

A particularly explicit moment of the narrator's movement into this liminal time occurs early on in part two of *Swann's Way*. The passage also illustrates, as we shall see, Proust's indebtedness to Bergson, particularly to Bergson's repeated metaphor of duration as an inner melody. It is the moment when Swann, visiting Odette at the Verdurins', listens to a pianist playing "the little phrase by Vinteuil that was like the anthem of their love":

> He would begin with the sustained violin tremolos that are heard alone for a few measures, occupying the entire foreground, then all of a sudden they seemed to move away and, as in those paintings by Pieter de Hooch, which assume greater depth because of the narrow frame of a half-open door, away in the distance, in a different color, in the velvet of an interposed light, the little phrase would appear, dancing, pastoral, interpolated, episodic, belonging to another world. It rippled past, simple and immortal, distributing here and there the gifts of its grace, with the same ineffable smile.[21]

The movement from continuous linear time to time's deviation from established patterns; from "measures" and "foreground" (*premier plan*) to an experience so extraordinary as to call forth a catalogue of adjectives, a painterly comparison, and a flowery metaphor—none of which, as Swann repeatedly insists, assuring him of conveying the experience with precision or rightness—replays itself in the analogy to Pieter de Hooch's painting, in which "the little phrase" has unexpectedly slipped through the half-open door to perform its magic; it occurs "in the velvet of an interposed light," as in the twilight of waking. But the moment passes unnoticed; "... it passed so close and yet infinitely far away, though it was addressed to them it did not know them,"[22] which repeats the scene of waking and forgetting mentioned above; and there seems thus sadly missed in this experience of a sudden aesthetic eternity, an intimacy into which Swann and Odette are not invited.

Earlier on, Swann attributes his susceptibility to music's charms to his "ignorance of music" (as one might be ignorant of sleep) that nonetheless yields an impression "purely musical, immaterial, entirely original, irreducible to any other order of impression,"[23] a pleasure, he goes on, "impossible to describe, to recall, to name, ineffable." And because it is so un-nameable, so vexingly indescribable, memory, "like a laborer working to put down lasting foundations in the midst of the waves, by fabricating for us facsimiles of these fleeting phrases" eventually produces a "transcription" that provides an analysis of the musical piece, "its extent, its symmetrical groupings, its notation, its expressive value," all of which, however, predictably "is no longer pure music."[24] The facsimiles that memory here produces recall Kant's argument, as we have seen earlier, that the inner intuition of duration cannot be named without analogies to a progressing, spatial line; "the clear life of consciousness" extinguishes the "subdued light in which our mind had been resting."

Blanchot's notion of passing from one time into another is performed in these musical interludes from foreground to background, through Pieter de Hooch's half-open door, and from pure music to its analyzable notations. In each of their iterations, such experiences of "another time" effect in Swann, though he admits to leading a life of decadence and debauchery, an opening of his soul.[25] Such an opening of the soul, despite its mystical overtones, is for Proust nonetheless a carnal event, implying a sudden entrance into duration wherein, to repeat Merleau-Ponty's phrase, "soul and body find their articulation," and wherein "the past and the mind... pass into one another,"[26] and which resembles the fluid, unstable, intermingling of sleep and waking.

Apt and felicitous venue for such transport and transformation, the little phrase recurs unexpectedly in the closing pages of *Swann's Way*, initiated by the violin's "high notes on which it lingered as though waiting for something" and which aesthetic temporality—"the little phrase was addressing him"—conveys Swann back to "another world, of another order, ideas veiled in shadows, unknown, impenetrable to the intelligence."[27] The experience is veritably transformative—ethically, even spiritually. It is a textbook example of the Kantian aesthetic, awakening the *a priori* mental conditions for the experience of the beautiful that exist "latent in his mind"—as if in sleep—to disclose "what richness, what variety, is hidden unbeknownst to us within that great unpenetrated and disheartening darkness of our soul which we take for emptiness and nothingness."[28] Here, towards the end of Swann's frantic, increasingly disillusioned pursuit of his love of Odette—which pursuit we might read as the doomed (sometimes tedious) linear temporality of the novel's plot—the alterity of the beautiful inserts itself like a supersensible visitation—recalling its allegorical enactment by various animals in Bishop—here proffered by "some explorer of the invisible ... to bring it, from that divine world to which he has access, to shine for a few moments above ours."[29]

Time's absence

Furnished with an exquisitely receptive soul, Marcel encounters the enchantment of time's absence on several occasions in the first part of the novel where similar transformative scenes as the one with the *madeleine* recur. In one of these examples, Marcel, having fallen behind on a family outing in Combray, "had to run to rejoin my father and grandfather, who were calling me," but his good intentions to obey their calls are thwarted when he is yet again detained and confesses, "I found it all humming with the smell of hawthorns."[30]

But though I remained there in front of the hawthorns, breathing in, bringing into the presence of my thoughts, which did not know what to do with it, then losing and finding again their invisible and unchanging smell, absorbing myself in the rhythm that tossed their flowers here and there with youthful high spirits and at unexpected intervals like certain intervals in music, they offered me the same charm endlessly and with an inexhaustible profusion, but without letting me study it more deeply, like the melodies you replay a hundred times in succession without descending further into their secrets.[31]

The main focus—Marcel's lingering—is notably not the main clause of the sentence above though it is its chief verbal concern; and the main clause, "they offered me the same charm," slowed by illustration and detail, cannot be studied. What is also beyond comprehension—Marcel's experience—is grammatically subsidiary, both in the English translation and in the French original. His lingering before the hedge of hawthorns runs its course beneath or outside the official temporality of his father's and grandfather's waiting for him—and by implication outside a traditional nineteenth-century literary tradition. His lingering happens, after all, in what Proust likens to an "unexpected interval" in music, a minute space of silence, a mysterious interruption of a linear progression of sound and sense.

Meanwhile Marcel is absorbed by what is described as a veritably overwhelming synesthetic experience that threatens to overwhelm the syntax of Proust's sentence itself—the effluence of the hawthorns' invisible smell, the sensuous tossing of their flowers and their irresistible charm, all of which compose, in concert, the melody—the interlude—of his lingering. That melody in turn—reminding us again of Bergson's melody of duration—is throughout described as an experience involving physical and mental faculties alike: a remaining (*rester*), a breathing (*respirer*), a consciousness (*porter devant ma pensée*), an absorbtion in rhythms (*m'unir au rythme*), and a mental dwelling as in the intervals of a melody—all ultimately inaccessible to thought or study, and yet all accumulating to a shape and form that define the writing of Marcel Proust—a writing that apprehends from the rhythm of the hawthorns the rhythm of writerly attention.[32]

In other words, if Marcel's father or grandfather had sternly demanded a good reason for the boy's lingering, Marcel might well have had to postpone such an explanation until the writing of *A la recherche du temps perdu*. Proust admits somewhat coyly in parentheses the postponement of his comprehension of his childhood memories' vocational significance right after the tasting of the *madeleine*: "(though I did not yet know and had to put off to much later discovering why this memory made me so happy.)"[33] The deferment of this discovery constitutes yet another form of lingering on Proust's part, a lingering in turn imposed on the reader who according to Ricoeur would fully understand the implications of this deferment on "only a second reading, instructed by *Time Regained*."[34] While the requirement of such instruction seems to me somewhat severe, it is nonetheless conceivable that the reason why *In Search of Lost Time* is so forbiddingly voluminous is because the temporal length of its scenes of ecstatic lingering is as immeasurable as their meaning is unknowable and the task of the writer accordingly insurmountable. The hawthorns' charm is offered endlessly (*indéfiniment*), their profusion is inexhaustible (*inépuisable*) in a temporality as impenetrably *secret* as the glimpse of eternity that Gadamer claims works of art afford when we linger in them. Although in the second volume of *In Search of Lost Time*, Marcel reflects on this experience as "one that I seldom had occasion to revisit," he thinks of it as an "ungraspable reality... not just an aesthetic experience, but a heady desire, however fleeting, to live there forever."[35] Time's absence is here implied in the experience of the beautiful as evanescence and eternity at once.

As if in preparation for the scene in front of the hawthorns, the announcement of such an eternity occurs but one page before:

> We heard no sound of steps on the avenues. Dividing the height of an unknown tree, an invisible bird, contriving to make the day seem short, explored the surrounding solitude with one prolonged note, but received from it a retort so unanimous, a repercussion so redoubled by silence and immobility, that one felt it had arrested forever that moment which it had been trying to make pass more quickly.[36]

The passage is again structured by paradox: sound and silence, brevity and length, temporality and eternity, even as the binary of the paradox will be *sublated*. What this means is that contrary to the bird's un-Romantic intention to "make the day seem short," its "prolonged note" effects an echo that, "redoubled by silence and immobility," arrests the moment forever. Although the moment is *arrested*, it is arrested *forever* and will thus neither pass nor cease—it is at once cancellation and preservation, the paradox recalling Keats's very similar argument in "Ode on a Grecian Urn" where time likewise neither passes nor ceases.

Although the bird's anthropomorphized impatience in Proust's passage would shorten the day, its prolonged note awakens a veritable natural conspiracy that makes it resound forever. While its Romantic predecessors would have likely poured forth their souls in ecstasy or sat in darkness to cheer their own solitude with sweet sounds, Proust's bird is an ironic figure for the Post-Romantic poet. The passage amounts to an *ars poetica* that pits two temporalities against each other. If trying to "make the day seem short" instead arrests it forever, it is perhaps to signify that by analogy, trying to make a book "pass more quickly"— in the way novels are expected to be plotted, may instead make it a work of moments, all arrested forever. It depends on the quality of the prolonged note. In each instance of his untimely lingering, Marcel produces such a prolonged note.

At the beginning of *The Guermantes Way*, Proust thinks of such a prolonged note as occurring only in "rare moments" when "the dizzy whirl of daily life" slows and "we reflect upon the past in our daydreams and seek to grasp it by slowing down and suspending the perpetual motion in which we are carried along."[37] Proust's observation here accounts for the different temporalities of reading elicited by the novel. There is the dizzy whirl in which one rushes through (or skips, I shamefully admit) some tediously descriptive passages about the rites and rituals of "the vulgar herd of fashionable people,"[38] who, as we learn by the end of the novel, seem all along to have left the narrator as "cold" as they left us compared to "the hawthorns or the taste of a *madeleine*."[39] In the latter—though stumbling upon them in the dizzy whirl of Marcel's abundance of social obligations requires considerable readerly patience—one finds oneself delightfully arrested. The hawthorns and the *madeleine* here stand for the many unexpected lyric interludes, poetic reveries, or aesthetic reflections all of which usually broaden the narrative plot and autobiographical perspective by changing into the first person plural "we," thus drawing us into the confidence and experience of the narrator who promises, like Whitman, on each of such lyrical and leisurely retardations, what I assume you shall assume.

Lingering as vocation

Daydreamer of the beautiful, aspiring poet, pilgrim of the Méséglise way and the Guermantes way, Marcel develops a veritable knack in those enchanting early pages of *Swann's Way* for making his parents grow "impatient at the sight of me lingering behind."[40] "When he would dream in his solitude," Bachelard suggests, "the child knew an existence without bounds."[41] Although occasionally still waiting to be put to bed by his mother, Marcel experiences the temporality of lingering as an autonomous, aesthetic realm in which, in concert with that autonomy, lingering shapes a person's inclinations for the beautiful in vocational ways. "The seasons of memory are beautifying," writes Bachelard addressing that very vocational effect, "When one goes off dreaming to the bottom of their simplicity, into the very center of their value, the seasons of childhood are the seasons of the poet."[42] Thus, paradoxically at the moment when Marcel is distressed at finding he has "no aptitude for literature" and will never be "a famous writer," he encounters an aesthetic moment whose depth he cannot plumb and whose center he cannot find:

> ... my mind of its own accord, by a sort of inhibition in the face of pain, would stop thinking altogether about poems, novels, a poetic future on which my lack of talent forbade me to depend. Then, quite apart from all these literary preoccupations ... suddenly a roof, a glimmer of sun on a stone, the smell of the road would stop me because of a particular pleasure they gave me, and also because they seemed to be concealing, beyond what I could see, something which they were inviting me to come take and which despite my efforts I could not manage to discover.[43]

He will, of course, be a famous writer. "And thus," Bachelard again to the point here, "in his solitudes, from the moment he is master of his reveries, the child knows the happiness of dreaming which will later be the happiness of the poets."[44] "[I]f one advances confidently in the direction of his dreams, and endeavors to live the life he has imagined," Thoreau similarly notes in *Walden*, "he will meet with a success unexpected in common hours."[45] Marcel's early aesthetic experiences, despite his doubts and protestations, are deeply connected to his literary preoccupations. Precisely because of his childish lingering and stopping and falling behind, precisely because of what Bachelard would call his "slow childhood,"[46] his ability to "stay there, motionless, looking, breathing, trying to go with my thoughts beyond the image or the smell,"[47] he will become the writer of *In Search of Lost Time*.

Meanwhile, his futile attempts to discover something about, or to go beyond, the enchantment of such experiences continue once Marcel catches up with his grandfather. "I would try to find them again by closing my eyes,"[48] he says, and indeed, these same efforts to recall the roof, the brush of sun on the stone, the smell of the road are yet again undertaken "once I was back at the house"; but this time these aesthetic impressions merely "accumulate in my mind"[49] to form the "deep layers of my mental soil,"[50] as he will reflect a few pages later— in order to be unearthed in the very book I am reading.

Repeatedly (thus) Marcel's aesthetic enchantments prove so intense and so frustrating to his efforts to discover what they were concealing that an interruption, as when Rilke's child is "shaken back" into the sobering temporality of clocks, comes as a welcome relief from the mental and emotional burden of an experience unbearable to sustain over long periods of time and later impossible to keep to oneself:

> ... I would have liked to be able to sit down and stay there the whole day reading while I listened to the bells; because it was so lovely and tranquil that, when the hour rang, you would have said not that it broke the calm of the day, but that it relieved the day of what it contained....[51]

What relieved the day of what it contained is the hour that rings. But what the "it" is that the day contained in the depth of its tranquility remains as unspoken in the printed pages before us as it is for Marcel during the succession of those fine summer days. While the little boy erroneously thinks of these "impressions" as "tied to a particular object with no intellectual value or no reference to any abstract truth," Proust mentions the intellectual deficiencies of the objects Marcel ponders at this moment of self-doubt, I think, only to point out that the significance of his aesthetic experiences is precisely that at this stage in his life they seem to him to have no extrinsic value, such as is traditionally vested in intellectual or abstract truth. By those authoritative lights, the boy mistakenly concludes, he had lost all hope "of succeeding in becoming a writer and a poet someday."[52] What it is that the day contained will, in other words, have to be postponed until it will be endlessly examined, interrogated, and reconsidered in the seven volumes of *A la recherche du temps perdu*.

Like *du côté de Guermantes*, the path that follows the course of the Vivonne, we follow the pages of *Du côté de chez Swann* temporarily relieved of what the day contained until we find ourselves, two pages further on, face to face with yet another aesthetic object, this time a water lily caught in the mechanics of the flowing water whose tribulations remind Marcel—lingering behind—of Dante's souls "tormented ... indefinitely throughout eternity." Marcel's parents—playing the role of Virgil, who in Dante's *Commedia* repeatedly admonishes the aspiring poet to hurry and keep up with him—yet again call him out of his reverie[53]:

> Fortunately, my parents would call me, I would feel I did not have the tranquillity I needed at the moment for pursuing my search in a useful way, and that it would be better not to think about it

anymore until I was back home, and not to fatigue myself beforehand to no purpose. And so I would stop concerning myself with this unknown thing that was enveloped in a form or a fragrance....[54]

Marcel's encounters with nature and his repeated frustrations to decipher "this unknown thing" find an analogue in Kant's aesthetic theory where the experiences of the beautiful, in nature as in artistic forms, presuppose the mental calm embodied in lingering. While it is precisely the *incomprehensibility* of Marcel's encounters that can be said to elicit or necessitate the lyrical style of Proust's writing, it is inversely (or dialectically) the very indeterminacy of lyric poetry, its freedom from conceptual and utilitarian constraints, its unaccountability (to use a Stevensian term), that makes it a vehicle for the intuition of the kind of supersensible reality that Marcel intuits in "this unknown thing." What Kant—who moves and has his being in these cogitations—also hints at is that, beyond sense or understanding, the freedom and spontaneity of poetry, while provoking supersensible intuitions, also perilously court the irrational. Lyric brevity, like the brevity of aesthetic experiences, implies that their intensity and intimations either would be unbearable if not contained by poetic form[55] or interrupted by narrative necessities. Lawless freedom of the imagination, Kant writes, produces nothing but nonsense. The judgment of taste, he goes on, is the poet's discipline that prunes the wings of his imagination.[56] If Marcel hadn't lingered and fallen behind, he would never have become a famous writer; but likewise if his parents hadn't called him out of his reveries, we would have no novel. The dreamer must wake up from the opaline depths of the sea.

The opening of the soul

There are numerous moments in *Swann's Way* when we might feel deeply connected with Marcel's experience of an aesthetic event that, because of its insistent beckoning and signifying beyond his or our conceptual or mental capacities, welcomes an interruption that calls him and us back into comprehensible and useful domestic or quotidian tasks or appointments. (I, for example, am happily called at this very minute to reawaken the fire in the wood stove.) That the beautiful is here endured as a veritable burden, that the intensity of the calm and tranquility of this experience would be unbearable without interruption, explains at once why we have no interest in listening to the humming of life's depths, why lyrics are short, why they are intense, and why a writer's vocation extends far back into his childhood where the early inarticulate endurance precisely of such calm and tranquility initiates a calling never to end the efforts and frustrations of deciphering them.

The many lyric interludes in *Swann's Way,* especially in the Combray chapters, trace the continuance of this effort, a concern about things mysteriously "enveloped in a form or a fragrance"[57] like a lyric poem, like a *madeleine,* like a bank of hawthorns, like a water lily, like a musical phrase. They both set in motion and interrupt a narrative in which they are embedded, as lyric time is conventionally embedded in narrative time, as lingering is embedded in waiting, as the individual is embedded in history—and without which initiations and interruptions we would have no inkling that we *are* in time or in history. As we have seen in Woolf, in Proust, and as we shall see in Sebald, the intensity of these interludes threatens to overwhelm or subvert the temporal and narrative frame in which they were meant to be contained.

In spite of the relative brevity of these lyric or aesthetic interludes— though in the Combray chapters they may each cover a number of pages until Marcel is almost invariably called by voices from the realm of parental time and domestic sovereignty—we may imagine these interludes as a submerged flow of time that emerges periodically, like the humming of life's depth, like the melody of duration beneath the authoritative parental order. If the latter serves conventionally as the subject or tenor in a metaphor, and the interludes and episodes as mere ornaments or vehicle, then that precedence is here, as it is in *Mrs. Dalloway,* inverted. Thus, the visible, comprehensible structure of the narrative defined by seasons, days, and hours—merely bothered as it must be with plots and actions intermittently to inflame or appease our readerly impatience—is here only thinly imposed on more essential "vicissitudes" and "episodes"; it is not the plot (whatever that might be in Proust's novel), but precisely the "dancing, pastoral, interpolated, episodic, belonging to another world"[58] (as Swann experiences pure music) that are the writer's—and the reader's—pleasure.

Shortly before the end of the second Combray chapter, Proust concludes that it is these vicissitudes and episodes, not history but poetry, not what was but what is possible, not time but duration, that constitute "our intellectual life"; our intellectual life "progresses within us imperceptibly" and "the truths ... that have opened new paths to us, we had been preparing to discover for a long time; but we did so without knowing it."[59] Since even "houses, roads, avenues are as fleeting, alas, as the years,"[60] what survives stone paths, walkers on those paths, the memory of those walkers, indeed what survives, we might add, the fastidious prattle of the morbidly degenerate aristocracy in the mansions and drawing rooms of Proust's work, is merely

> ... that child dreaming ... that bit of garden ... the fragrance of hawthorn ... a sound of echoless steps on the gravel of a path, a bubble formed against a water plant by the current of the stream and bursting immediately—my exaltation has borne them along with it and managed to carry them across so many years....[61]

It is the most transient, the least noticed, the most evanescent, but also the immeasurable, the inimitable, the non-repeatable that constitutes the "deep layers of my mental soil, as the firm ground on which I still stand."[62] The firm ground is, of course, Benjamin's everyday hour, "the hour that was most his own."

It is a great paradox—this hour that was most his own. For what is deep must nonetheless be transient; what is firm must nonetheless be fragile. Towards the end of *Swann's Way* we find the same transient, fragile temporality briefly enjoyed by Swann when he listens to the last reverberations of the little phrase from Vinteuil's sonata, whose melody is nothing other than a musical transcription of the child dreaming, that bit of garden, the fragrance of hawthorn: "Swann did not dare to move and would have made all the other people be still too, as if the slightest motion might compromise the fragile, exquisite, and supernatural magic that was so close to vanishing."[63]

We who have no aptitude for literature and will never be famous writers, must learn, nonetheless, to linger in our waiting. Our resistance by which we oppose the time-is-money culture will remain unspectacular, indeed literally so, in that it is largely obscurely performed in the breath drawn at an open window, in small rooms before paintings, in sudden clearings in the woods, in languid moments on Tuesday afternoons, perhaps in the reading of poems or in the writing of prose passages (such as these), perhaps in bus stations and hospital waiting rooms, or at the curb of busy streets. One doesn't need an app or a degree for it. But one is strangely humanized by it. It opens one's soul.

Notes

1. Benjamin, *Illuminations*, 203 (translation slightly edited).
2. Ibid.
3. An excellent discussion of this issue is in Gian Balsamo, "The Fiction of Marcel Proust's Autobiography," *Poetics Today* 28. 4 (2007).
4. Proust, *Swann's Way*, 45.
5. Ibid., 47.
6. Proust, *In the Shadow of Young Girls in Flower*, 222.
7. Blanchot, *The Space of Literature*, 60.
8. Barthes, *The Grain of the Voice*, 343.

9 Barthes, *The Pleasure of the Text*, 36.
10 Blanchot, *The Space of Literature*, 265.
11 Ibid.
12 Ibid.
13 Ibid.
14 Proust, *Swann's Way*, 46.
15 *The Divine Comedy of Dante Alighieri: Inferno*, trans. Allen Mandelbaum (New York: Bantam Books, 1982), 3.
16 Blanchot, *The Space of Literature*, 265.
17 Proust, *Swann's Way*, 47.
18 Ibid.
19 Ibid., 3, 5.
20 Marcel Proust, *The Guermantes Way*, trans. Mark Treharne (New York: Penguin, 2002), 331–32.
21 Proust, *Swann's Way*, 226.
22 Ibid., 227.
23 Ibid., 216.
24 Ibid., 217.
25 Ibid., 216, 245.
26 Merleau-Ponty, *Signs*, 185.
27 Proust, *Swann's Way*, 358, 361, 362.
28 Ibid., 363.
29 Ibid., 364.
30 Ibid., 140.
31 Ibid., 141.
32 Cf. Susanne Langer as quoted in Stewart, *The Poet's Freedom*, who describes the non-discursive forms of art making as "the rhythms of life, organic, emotional and mental (the rhythm of attention is an interesting link among them all)" (57).
33 Proust, *Swann's Way*, 47.
34 Though Ricoeur qualifies this requirement by granting "the reader with a keen ear" the possibility of accomplishing this task "on a first reading"; *Time and Narrative*, vol. 2, 136.
35 Proust, *In the Shadow of Young Girls in Flower*, 300–301.
36 Proust, *Swann's Way*, 140.
37 Proust, *The Guermantes Way*, 6.
38 Ibid., 24.
39 Ibid., 549.
40 Proust, *Swann's Way*, 177.
41 Bachelard, *Poetics of Reverie*, 100.
42 Ibid., 117.
43 Proust, *Swann's Way*, 182.
44 Bachelard, *Poetics of Reverie*, 99.
45 Thoreau, *Walden, Civil Disobedience and Other Writings.* 217.
46 Bachelard, *Poetics of Reverie*, 109.
47 Proust, *Swann's Way*, 182.
48 Ibid.
49 Ibid., 183.
50 Ibid., 188.
51 Ibid., 170.

52 Ibid., 183.
53 Ibid., 173.
54 Ibid., 183.
55 Kant, *Kritik der Urteilskraft*, § 43.
56 Ibid., § 50.
57 Proust, *Swann's Way,* 183.
58 Ibid., 226.
59 Ibid., 187.
60 Ibid., 444.
61 Ibid., 188.
62 Ibid.
63 Ibid., 365.

10 The weight of Sebald's time

The draining of the world

"To set one's name to a work gives no one a title to be remembered, for who knows how many of the best men have gone without a trace?" This sobering phrase from the seventeenth-century physician and writer Thomas Browne, quoted in W.G. Sebald's *The Rings of Saturn*, should serve as a warning against any writer's ambition to survive stone sidewalks and curbs, pedestrians on those sidewalks, and the memory of those pedestrians. And yet Sebald's prose, set in motion by his astoundingly indefatigable lingering over vanished and vanishing lives, seems to have its *raison d'être* in nothing less than the defiance of any caveat such as Browne's. In his novel *Austerlitz*, for example, Sebald laments

> ... how little we can hold in mind, how everything is constantly lapsing into oblivion with every extinguished life, how the world is, as it were, draining itself, in that the history of countless places and objects which themselves have no power of memory is never heard, never described or passed on.[1]

Neither nostalgic nor sentimental nor fanciful, the wanderings of this narrator in search of vestiges of extinguished life across rural or urban sites mostly in northern and central Europe mirror the associative, spellbinding drift of his prose, which despite the asceticism of its narrator is luxurious and expansive, and wherein the obsessively inventoried fragments of countries and cultures in decline seem to be held back from oblivion by the meticulous, patient slowness of Sebald's prose.

"[T]he movements of all the travelers," we learn in *Austerlitz*, are "surveyed from the central position occupied by the clock in Antwerp Station" which "prescribed that we could hasten through the gigantic spaces separating us from each other."[2] While his narrators are throughout subject to the haste, even panic, that such surveillance exerts on them, Sebald's work, as Thomas Steinfeld insightfully explains, is a "slowing down, 'deceleration' (*Entschleunigung*) would be a better word for this singular attempt of holding still (*Innehalten*) in deeply reflective world-piety."[3] Sebald's project, writes Klaus R. Scherpe similarly, assumes a sense of time that longs to rest.[4]

Mesmerizing in its intimacy and particularity, every page performs a protracted lingering upon lives and things that time, slowed by the author's languid, vigilant attention, slowly devours. Every page of his books opens like a drawer in a cabinet of natural and cultural curiosities whose contents are painstakingly catalogued:

> The servants who kept all in good order, the butlers, coachmen, chauffeurs, gardeners, cooks, sempstresses and chambermaids, have long since gone. ... The velvet curtains and crimson blinds are faded, the settees and armchairs sag, the stairways and corridors ... are full of bygone paraphernalia. A camphorwood chest which may once have accompanied a former occupant of the house on a tour of duty to Nigeria or Singapore now contains old croquet mallets and wooden balls, golf clubs, billiard cues and tennis racquets, most of them so small they might have been intended for children, or have shrunk in the course of the years. The walls are hung with copper kettles, bedpans, hussars' sabres....[5]

Sebald's re-imaginings of lives long past, his amused consideration of the size of the objects he lists, his whimsical contemplation about whether their smallness might indicate their intended use, or whether their shrinking might be due to the passage of time, all of it leaves us with a melancholy that is wistful—almost witty, poignant—almost sad. These complex emotional qualities of Sebald's prose are exemplified in a sentence where he considers shrinking (of all things) a wholly natural process: "for the experience of death ... diminishes us, just as a piece of linen shrinks when you first wash it."[6] The sincerity of the phrase, strangely, seems not to suffer even as the comparison of life and death to the shrinking of linen confounds by its comical incongruity. In the curiously testimonial qualities of such bygone junk (*Kram*) as old croquet mallets and wooden balls, golf clubs, billiard cues, and tennis racquets there linger, shyly but persistently, traces of human lives, traces of trauma, traces of an existential significance, albeit shrunk like washed linen, albeit droll in their trifling particularity, for which Sebald has no better theology than the intimate, fortuitous stories and histories that all of his books tell.

The temporality of trauma

What fuels Sebald's narrative compulsions in his four major novels—but nowhere more self-evidently than in *Austerlitz*, whose eponymous character seeks to retrace his exile as a four-and-half-year-old in a 1939 Kindertransport to England and to uncover his parents' disappearance in the Holocaust—is the trauma of the past, or the past as trauma, the very passage of time itself, which Sebald frequently allegorizes in train journeys, extended walking tours, or aimless wandering.

Strolling through the city of The Hague in *The Rings of Saturn* for example, Sebald's narrator suddenly "glimpsed the wooden rack on which perhaps a hundred pairs of well-worn shoes had been placed beside and above one another." The moment refuses, for a time, integration into official ledgers. For the accidental discovery of this wooden rack of shoes amounts to what Sebald calls—we don't know why— "an unforgettable moment that seemed to exist outside time."[7] While Sebald's claim will initially seem incongruous, upon reflection— by which Sebald transfers his own lingering to his reader—it will appear overdetermined. The overdetermination likely comes about by Sebald's encounters with the shoes of Jewish victims of the Holocaust, abandoned and stacked "above one another" in heaps in museums, and which traumatic recall here delays and elaborates, and again complicates and confounds both our reading and the narrator's experience. On the visual page, the reverberations of the trauma last only briefly; in the anticlimax of the very next sentence beginning with, "Only later did I see the minaret," the moment seems at least to this reader almost immediately forgotten, or—upon reflection—deflected and repressed. To the writer, the contextual explanation that the shoes belonged to the worshippers in the mosque came, he reports, "only later," while he "walked around" presumably for "an hour or more" in a section of the city that had under the influence of the traumatic encounter transformed to a "somehow extraterritorial part of town."[8] Here then, we intuit the unforgettable moment as exerting a power capable of the kind of defamiliarization of the blandly quotidian that is the hallmark of Sebald's writing, a writing whose slowness is mirrored in the reader's hesitations, delayed understanding, and adjustments.

The scene with the shoes in *The Rings of Saturn* is foreshadowed in Sebald's first novel, *Vertigo*, where the narrator, aimlessly as usual, wanders through the city of Vienna and is "shocked by the sight of my shoes, which were literally falling apart." That same night the trauma of the Holocaust returns when Sebald's narrator hears, through the windows of his hotel room, emanating from the Jewish community center, "The voices of singing children, and now in front of me my tattered and, as it seemed, ownerless shoes. Heaps of shoes and snow piled high—with these words in my head I lay down."[9] The "snow piled high" in the context of the heaps of shoes may strike us as odd. It is indeed not until *Austerlitz,* Sebald's last novel, where the narrator is waiting for an eye-appointment, that we learn that snow apparently has anesthetic properties representing "my childhood wish for everything to be snowed over."[10]

That this trauma after its initial appearance in *Vertigo* would repeat itself years later in another European city and in another book, *The Rings of Saturn*, and then again in another book, *Austerlitz*, speaks to the temporality of delay and repetition of trauma itself, both delay and repetition making the trauma's occurrence as unpredictable as it happens in the three novels. Evidently, the measurable time of "an hour or more" of wandering around in The Hague does not resolve the traumatic encounter. The trauma is borne outside of measurable hours in an immeasurable temporality where it is as unforgettable and interminable as the writing it engenders.

The temporality of the photograph

The *measure* of time is wholly irrelevant to the *depth* of an experience, traumatic or not. Nor is history cause or measure of trauma but the a-historical *punctum* of the event of the trauma itself. In *The Rings of Saturn,* in the same city of The Hague where he discovered the rack of shoes, Sebald's narrator remembers the following scene that occurs during a rainstorm:

> ... in the shelter of an overhanging willow, I saw a solitary mallard, motionless on the garish green surface of the water. This image emerged from the darkness, for a fraction of a second, with such perfect clarity that I can still see every individual willow leaf, the myriad green scales of duckweed, the subtlest nuances in the fowl's plumage, and even the pores in the lid closed over its eye.[11]

Here the slowness of lingering is evidently in no way defined by or dependent on the "fraction of a second" during which it yields a vision of the bird's delicate, brief, beautiful appearance. Sebald's remark "I can still see" extracts this moment out of time; the stillness of the Sabbath gaze restores with "perfect clarity" the bird's otherwise invisible beauty, so that, one might say, this creature will not vanish without a trace as do the best men in Sir Thomas Browne's phrase. The meticulous detail in the observation conveys a gentle empathy. In its very brevity, the scene with the mallard composes a *chronotope*, a room, a stanza, a site of duration, as I put it earlier, where duration has transformed to space, where historic or epic time, as Scherpe puts it, converts to private space or the format of the anecdote.[12] Here, the scene has the temporality of a photograph, the shutter of the camera opening for a fraction of a second to arrest the image of the motionless mallard.

It is with some surprise, since Sebald collaborated with his translators, that in the German original, *Die Ringe des Saturn*, the narrator remembers not "a solitary mallard" but a pair of them (*Entenpaar*), a recollection that, by contrast, emphasizes the narrator's own solitary perspective; and the translation's "I can still see" conveys as certainty of what is in German slightly more conjectural *das ich jetzt noch … zu sehen vermeine*,[13] (literally, that I still think I'm seeing). The translation thus overexposes, as it were, the gritty, very slightly faded quality of the narrator's memory. Here is a lineated rendition of the passage:

> In the shelter of the hanging
> branches of a weeping willow
> I saw a pair of mallards,
> motionless on the surface
> of the water covered with a garish
> green film of duckweed. I can
> still almost see every single
> willow leaf, the intricate
> shades in the fowls' plumage,
> even the tiny specks of
> the pores in their lids lowered
> over their eyes.

The intimacy of this glimpse into the nuanced detail of this photographic image—whose poetic version (in my translation), I hope, might reflect the syllabic meter and lineation of Sebald's poems—is repeated throughout Sebald's work; the same intimate specificity occurs for example when Austerlitz, riding a small elevator with Tereza Ambrosová in Prague, detects "a gentle pulsation in the curve of a blue vein beneath the skin of her right temple, almost as fast as the throbbing in a lizard's throat when it lies motionless on a rock in the sun."[14] The delicate, fragile embodiment of time in the pulsing of the vein implies the comparability of all things; one may find oneself fortuitously a mallard in The Hague, a lizard on a rock in the sun, an ownerless shoe in a stack of shoes, or no less surreal and Kafkaesque, a human in an elevator in Prague.

The duration of knowledge

Although Roland Barthes, in his moving reflections about photography in *Camera Lucida*, insists that no writing can convey "the certainty" that a photograph can,[15] he subsequently describes the aesthetic reception of the photograph as analogous to the reading of a text. Barthes' claim that the photograph "cannot be penetrated" and that "I can only sweep it with my glance"[16] recalls the well-known binary set up in his famous essay "The Death of the Author" between the conventional *work* that invites piercing and deciphering, and the *text* that can only be disentangled and ranged over.

Nonetheless, in *Camera Lucida*, Barthes is repeatedly tempted precisely to pierce photographs and thus to subvert the idea of the photograph as text: "Since Photography (this is its *noeme*) *authenticates* the existence of a certain being, I want to discover that being in the photograph completely." But the desire for complete discovery is predictably not to be granted: the photograph "can correspond to my fond desire only by something inexpressible .... This something is what I call the *air*, (the expression, the look)."[17] A few pages earlier Barthes attempts to explain the process by which "something inexpressible" that is nonetheless "the expression, the look" can be known:

> If I like a photograph, if it disturbs me, I linger over it. What am I doing, during the whole time I remain with it? I look at it, I scrutinize it, as if I wanted to know more about the thing or the person it represents. Lost in the depths of the Winter Garden, my mother's face is vague, faded. In a first impulse, I exclaimed: "There she is! She's really there! At last there she is!" Now I claim to know—and to be able to say adequately—why, in what she consists. I want to outline the loved face by thought, to make it into the unique field of an intense observation; I want to enlarge this face in order to see it better, to understand it better, to know its truth...I decompose, I enlarge, and, so to speak, I *retard*, in order to have time to *know* at last.[18]

A photograph, so Barthes seems to suggest, reveals itself in elaboration ("I enlarge") and retardation ("I *retard*")—Bergson's terms for time. But if a photograph requires the same slow, patient reading as a postmodern text, a "ranging over" as Barthes suggests in "The Death of the Author," then here again Barthes' desire "to *know* at last" seems impatiently to subvert that hermeneutic. Barthes reiterates the desire for final knowledge when he says that "to scrutinize means to turn the photograph over, to enter into the paper's depth, to reach the other side." But again predictably, the impulse to pierce and decipher the photograph of the Winter Garden proves impossible, and the chapter ends, "Such is the Photograph: it cannot *say* what it lets us see."[19]

What then does it mean for Barthes to insist "I *retard*, in order to have time to *know* at last"? Does it mean that knowledge of a photograph is "to have time to know at last"? Is such knowledge not knowledge of a thing but *of the time of looking*? Is looking knowing? If so, what we know of another being in a photograph is not something that could be acquired *through* a photograph; it is not a *telos* waiting to be revealed by means and mediation of the photograph. Instead, what we know of another being in a photograph is what is in our looking, lingering, and remembering, such as repeats itself in Sebald's phrase "I can still almost see," and which seeing, like his writing, is ever incomplete in the "almost." But nothing can be known other than the seeing, nothing other than the writing, nothing other than the "almost." Our seeing acknowledges the seeing of which the photograph itself is an image and an expression.

A good photograph is slow; it lengthens the brevity of which it is a picture, which is why Barthes thinks that photographs are of *what has been*, which is ongoing time in the continuous present perfect. In the moment of the clicking of the shutter, photographs record "the noise of Time"; cameras are "clocks for seeing."[20] Sebald, one might say, writes not with a pen (or a keyboard) but with a camera. In a felicitous paragraph by Bachelard, finally, Sebald's and Barthes' photographic visions seem to fuse:

> It is reverie which provides the time to accomplish this aesthetic composition. It surrounds the real with enough light for the picture taking to be ample. In the same way, brilliant photographers know how to give duration to their snapshots, very exactly as *duration of reverie*. The poet does the same thing.[21]

The many photographs in Sebald's work convey the duration of reverie. In their gritty, black-and-white appearance, they seem to reach us as from a world long gone; or, they speak to us as if they were photographs not of the external world but of the internal world of dream. They are photographs of dreams at the moment of awakening. They literalize the temporality of Sebald's prose in which, as in a photograph, we "can still almost see" what would otherwise have vanished without a trace, but the photographs' somewhat antiquated, black-and-white quality also suggests the forgetting of the dream at the moment of awakening, the slow vanishing of the traces of the living in the darkening, narrowing passage of time.

The narrowing of time

Luisa Lanzberg, in *The Emigrants*, is such a vanishing trace. In her memoir, Sebald reports, she arrives at a moment when her childhood appears to her "as if it had been open-ended in time, in every direction—indeed, as if it were still going on, right into these lines I am now writing." The fact that one needs to remind oneself that "these lines I am now writing" are Luisa's not Sebald's—a confusion of identity, voice, and authorship that pervades Sebald's work and is exemplified most notably in the confusion about the identity of the little boy on the title page of *Austerlitz* [22]—intimates a close kinship between Lanzberg's and Sebald's writing. Immediately in the next sentence, Luisa realizes that "in reality, as I know only too well, childhood ended in January 1905" after which the years up until her marriage in 1921 marked "a path that grew narrower day by day." These years, she recalls, are "difficult to think back" and "affected my ability to take things in."[23] While the potential of her memoir-writing is open-ended and multi-directional, the reality of the years to come weighs and narrows. The doom of Luisa's life is the weight of time in Sebald's writing; it comments on his struggle as a novelist against the might of time—the open-ended versus the narrow, the present versus the past, remembering versus forgetting, duration versus time. Luisa's doom individualizes what W.S. Merwin has beautifully called "the inconsolable sorrow of history" that permeates Sebald's work.[24]

The Rings of Saturn records a similar narrowing of time. It opens with the narrator's sense of delightful ease while walking in the county of Suffolk; but exactly to the day one year after he commenced his wanderings (*Dahinwandern*), he is admitted to a hospital "overwhelmed by the feeling that the Suffolk expanses … had now shrunk once and for all to a single, blind, insensate spot."[25] The sudden shrinking of space announces the tendency of time to narrow, diminish, shrink (like washed linen), and drain, against which Sebald marshals his astoundingly inexhaustible efforts, almost resembling the obsessions of a hoarder, to resist the lapsing of all lives and things into oblivion. "How strange it is," he writes in *Vertigo*, "to be standing leaning against the current of time."[26]

The descent into time

In the opening pages of *Campo Santo*, published posthumously, Sebald finds himself, as he often does in his narratives, with "a little time" in Ajaccio, Corsica, during which

The weight of Sebald's time 101

> I wandered through the streets feeling carefree and at ease, now and then going into one of the dark, tunnel-like entrances of buildings to read the names of their unknown inhabitants on the metal letter boxes with a certain rapt attention, trying to imagine what it would be like to live in one of these stone citadels, occupied to my life's end solely with the study of time past and passing.[27]

The narrator's strolling through the streets of Ajacco and his spontaneous entries of buildings perform the wandering, the seemingly aimless *Dahinwandern* of Sebald's prose, its sudden redirections and deflections, its compulsive uncoverings and recoverings of unknown inhabitants. The stone citadel to which he has retired in his fantasy to become a student of time past and passing is a metaphor for the book we are reading:

> But since we can none of us really live entirely withdrawn into ourselves, and must all have some more or less significant design in view, my wishful thinking about a few last years with no duties of any kind soon gave way to a need to fill the present afternoon somehow, and so I found myself, hardly knowing how I came there, in the entrance hall of the Musée Fesch, with notebook and pencil and a ticket in my hand.[28]

The book we are reading is, in other words, not about some more or less significant design, nor does it simply fill the present afternoon in which I happen to be reading it on this rainy day during the COVID pandemic. Sebald's visit to the museum turns out to be a descent into time past and passing as we witness it in all of Sebald's books; his descent commences with the lingerer's initial "rapt attention" to the names of "unknown inhabitants" in the museum's collection, then focuses on a seventeenth-century portrait by Pietro Paolini of a woman with

> ... large, melancholy eyes ... [who] wears a dress the color of the night, which does not stand out from the surrounding darkness even by suggestion and is thus really invisible, and yet it is present in every fold and drape of its fabric. She wears a string of pearls around her neck. Her right arm protectively embraces her small daughter, who stands in front of her turning sideways, toward the edge of the picture, but with her grave face, upon which the tears have only just dried, turned toward the observer in a kind of silent challenge.[29]

It is as if in this intimate encounter with the portrait of a mother with child, Sebald had entered through a dark tunnel-like entrance "one of these stone citadels" mentioned at the beginning. And as in Bachelard's notion of the redemptive potential of lingering, the closed frame of the portrait, like the solitary time of Sebald's lingering, here prove to be transformative: "I stood in front of this double portrait for a long time, seeing in it, as I thought at the time, an annulment of all the unfathomable misfortune of life."[30] But in its framed immobility, the painting performs not just a redemptive erasure or annulment of misfortune but also its preservation, a suspension, a lingering of all the unfathomable misfortune of life. It is in the woman's dress, in its simultaneous invisibility and yet its visibility in the folds and drapes of its fabric; it is on the daughter's cheeks, dried of tears both present and absent; and it is finally in the silence of her face turned emphatically towards the observer where this temporal paradox of annulment and preservation plays itself out. The painting is a painting of time and of all the misfortune time erases and of all the misfortune time preserves. It is a painterly rendition of a Greek tragedy's sublation of trauma.

In Sebald's visit to the Musée Fesch, the *preservation* of misfortune is sustained and endured in the "long time" of the visitor's meditation before the painting. In a similar scene in *Austerlitz*, Austerlitz visits the Rembrandt exhibition in the Rijksmuseum in Amsterdam and

> ... stood for a long time looking at a small painting measuring at most nine by twelve inches ... which according to its label showed the Flight into Egypt, although he could make out neither Mary and Joseph, nor the child Jesus, nor the ass, but only a tiny flicker of fire in the middle of the gleaming black varnish of the darkness which, said Austerlitz, he could see in his mind's eye to this day.[31]

Even when they remain indecipherable, even when prompted by a mere "tiny flicker of fire"—such as burns the photographic image onto the film—moments of lingering preserve things in their very vanishing, like a photograph. In the experience of lingering, then, one might be initiated into an event that despite its seemingly minimal affect burns itself into one's "mind's eye." Such discrepancy between a cause and its effect occurs again at an unexpected moment on the same day in *Santo Campo* when Sebald's narrator bends over the counter to the cashier of Casa Bonaparte and finds himself face to face with "one of those moments strangely experienced in slow motion that are sometimes remembered years later."[32]

Sebald's surprise at "hardly knowing how I came there" when he enters the Musée Fesch as well as his narrative is, as we have seen, a recurrent experience of the person who finds himself in the untimely temporality of lingering. It is the incitement or inspiration as much of Proust's as of Sebald's writing, as it is of poetry, most famously dramatized in Dante's *Inferno* in which opening lines Dante confesses,

> When I had journeyed half of our life's way,
> I found myself within a shadowed forest,
> for I had lost the path that does not stray.
> ...
> I cannot clearly say how I had entered
> the wood; I was so full of sleep....[33]

Scenes of disorientation occur frequently in Sebald's work. In the opening pages of the "Max Ferber" chapter of *The Emigrants*, the narrator is "overcome by such a sense of aimlessness and futility that I would go out, purely in order to preserve an illusion of purpose,"[34] which determination is repeated in his realization in *Campo Santo*, quoted above, that we "must all have some more or less significant design in view"—a version of Dante's "path that does not stray." As if his ears had been burning, and as if to confirm such literary allusion, Dante strangely and quite serendipitously makes an appearance in *Vertigo* when in a kind of delirium, the narrator lost in Gonzagagasse "thought I recognized the poet Dante," but fails to catch up with his vision and experiences "a feeling of vertigo," the word fortuitously announcing the writing of a book with the title, *Vertigo*.[35] Presumably then, Sebald encounters the writing of *Vertigo*, like Dante, full of sleep.

In that book, to soothe his nervous ailments, Sebald's narrator enters a park during his travels in northern Italy:

> I travelled as far as Verona, and there, having taken a room at the Golden Dove, went immediately to the Giardino Giusti, a long-standing habit of mine. There I spent the early
> ...
> hours of the afternoon lying on a stone bench below a cedar tree. I heard the soughing of the breeze among the branches and the delicate sound of the gardener raking the gravel paths between the low box hedges, the subtle scent of which still filled the air even in autumn. I had not experienced such a sense of well-being for a long time.[36]

The visitor's idling on a bench in the Giardino Giusti during the early hours of the afternoon is somewhat exceptional in a book otherwise rife with recurring episodes of panic, fear, and hectic sudden departures and hurried train rides. The photograph of Sebald's admissions ticket to the park, abruptly inserted into this text between the words "early" and "hours," indicated by the ellipsis above, appears to mimic the interruption, or hesitation, of time itself. In the sounds and scents that reach this visitor in his calm and that would have been inaudible and imperceptible in the surrounding city, the visitor's sense of well-being, meanwhile, recalls Bachelard's sense of the therapeutic effects of reverie. As the narrative progresses and Sebald's traveler finds himself mostly bereft of the felicitous properties of such lyrical interludes, it is the delicate and subtle qualities of his experience in the park—and it is eminently an experience of the beautiful—that shape the language that guides this writer in each of his books "to probe my somewhat imprecise recollections of those fraught and hazardous days."[37]

The lingering that life is

It is difficult to imagine that Austerlitz, who has "never owned a clock of any kind," and for whom "certain moments had no beginning or end,"[38] here does not speak for the author of *Austerlitz* himself:

> And is not human life in many parts of the earth governed to this day less by time than by the weather, and thus by an unquantifiable dimension which disregards linear regularity, does not progress constantly forward but moves in eddies, is marked by episodes of congestion and irruption, recurs in ever-changing form, and evolves in no one knows what direction? Even in a metropolis ruled by time like London, said Austerlitz, it is still possible to be outside time.... The dead are outside time, the dying and all the sick at home or in hospitals, and they are not the only ones, for a certain degree of personal misfortune is enough to cut us off from the past and the future.[39]

The narrowness of time, the more or less significant design, or the linear regularity of London time construct a past, present, and future wherein we devise form, memory, and vision. Governed, however, not by linear plot but by the weather (so to speak), the rhizomatic style of Sebald's novels—clearly alluded to in Austerlitz's exclamations—transports us outside time into the intimate temporality of the dead, the dying, the sick, and all those exiled from time. Barred from the past and all the future, they inhabit the eternity of Dante's inferno, that other, darker, dimension of lingering that we mean when we say that someone lingers in suffering and dying, and which expression accentuates both the solitude that lingering is and its unbearable infinity. "There, the present is without end," Blanchot notes, "separated from every other present by an inexhaustible and empty infinite, the very infinite of suffering, and thus dispossessed of any future: a present without end and yet impossible as a present." Suffering, he adds a little later, is an outside time, "a time neither abiding nor granting the simplicity of a dwelling place."[40]

Since "a certain degree of personal misfortune" awaits most of us, most of us at one time or another sooner or later move into that temporality "outside of time" that the lingerer shares with the dying and the dead. Tormented by the death and disappearance of his parents during the Holocaust, Austerlitz asserts later on in the novel that for him it was

> ... as if time did not exist at all, only various spaces interlocking ... between which the living and the dead can move back and forth as they like, and the longer I think about it the more it seems to me that we who are still alive are unreal in the eyes of the dead, that only occasionally, in certain lights and atmospheric conditions, do we appear in their field of vision.[41]

What if unbeknownst to ourselves, even on those strangely felicitous occasions—we would hardly know how we came there—perhaps under lime-tree bowers, in a sunny spot, within the shadowed forest, on God's handkerchief, in woods on a snowy evening, oblivious of such morbid vicinities and kinships—what if the enchantment of those moments outside of time resided in the light and atmospheric conditions by which we would have appeared in the dead's field of vision? Rilke and Whitman would entertain such possibilities.

When Gerald, in *Austerlitz*, recalls looking out at the Irish Sea as if it were a painting by J.M.W. Turner, it is precisely such conditions that permit his entrance into a blissful temporal exile:

> All forms and colors were dissolved in a pearl-gray haze; there were no contrasts, no shading anymore, only flowing transitions with the light throbbing through them, a single blur from which only the most fleeting of visions emerged, and strangely—I remember this well—it was the very evanescence of those visions that gave me, at the time, something like a sense of eternity.[42]

The sense of eternity derived from the merging of all distinctions and the uninterrupted flow of forms and colors recalls the immeasurable

106 The weight of Sebald's time

temporality of duration. It is no accident that this passage comes about in the context of a protracted study of moths, whose varieties are meticulously catalogued, and whose briefest of lives—in their beauty and sentience, for "[w]e are not alone in dreaming at night"[43]— embody the fleeting eternity of Gerald's aesthetic experience. On another occasion, such a vision of eternity, also paradoxically experienced as a mere fleeting moment, occurs in Austerlitz's experience of

> ... the last rays of the sun shining low through the moving branches of a hawthorn, until at last they were extinguished. There was something fleeting, evanescent about those sparse patterns appearing in constant succession on the pale surface, something which never went beyond the moment of its generation....[44]

Although measurable time asserts itself in the succession of the moving patterns and the cessation of the sun's light, the moment of lingering, though fleeting, evanescent, does not pass. It is a painted still-life.

For us who in our transience resemble moths, even eternity appears to be fleetingly brief. But it is in such eternities of duration that we experience the lingering that life is; and if so, our experience would explain our enchantments in the beautiful but perhaps also our desire to return to the metropolis ruled by time. Rilke deeply understood that such untimely experiences as lingering, which he calls authentic being, *Hiersein*, are shared with the dead. In the scene where the child wanders in this realm of "timeless / stillness" and has to be shaken back, Rilke adds, "Or that one dies and *is* it,"[45] which designates the timeless stillness as a realm wherein the dead, like Rilke's angels, move back and forth as they like. Sebald's work likewise moves irresistibly from lingering to lingering, from the brief eternities where one lingers as in an enchanting daydream towards that other lingering that we suffer in the solitude of our personal misfortune.

Notes

1 W.G. Sebald, *Austerlitz*, trans. Anthea Bell (New York: Modern Library, 2011), 24.
2 Ibid., 12.
3 Thomas Steinfeld, *Süddeutsche Zeitung*, December 17, 2001: "*Das wunderbare Unternehmen des Schriftstellers W.G. Sebald war die Verlangsamung – 'Entschleunigung' wäre der bessere Ausdruck für diesen einzigartigen Versuch des Innehaltens in hochreflektierter Weltfrömmigkeit.*" Many of Sebald's critics have commented on the slowness of his style.
4 Klaus R. Scherpe, "*Auszeit des Erzählens*: W.G. Sebalds Poetik der Beschreibung" in *Schreiben ex patria / Expatriate Writing* (Amsterdam: Quill,

2009): "*Sein Projekt einer Literatur der kleinen Form—der historischen Zeit im privaten Raum, der epischen Welt im Format der Anekdote—kommt einem Zeitempfinden entgegen, das ausruhen möchte*" (297).
5 Sebald, *The Rings of Saturn*, trans. Michael Hulse (New York: New Directions, 1998), 35.
6 Sebald, *Austerlitz*, 54.
7 Sebald, *The Rings of Saturn*, 81.
8 Ibid.; not, as some commentators have speculated, because the section was inhabited by Muslims.
9 Sebald, *Vertigo*, 37.
10 Sebald, *Austerlitz*, 37.
11 Sebald, *The Rings of Saturn*, 89.
12 Scherpe, "*Auszeit des Erzählens*," 297.
13 W.G. Sebald, *Die Ringe des Saturn* (Frankfurt: Fischer, 1997), 110.
14 Sebald, *Austerlitz*, 146.
15 Barthes, *Camera Lucida*, 85.
16 Ibid., 106.
17 Ibid., 107.
18 Ibid., 99.
19 Ibid., 100.
20 Ibid., 15.
21 Bachelard, *Poetics of Reverie*, 120.
22 Cf. James Wood, Introduction to *Austerlitz*, xiv; cf. also Marit MacArthur's review of *Across the Land and into the Water* in *The Yale Review* 1. 101. (2013).
23 Sebald, *The Emigrants*, 207–208.
24 From W.S. Merwin's blurb on *Austerlitz*.
25 Sebald, *The Rings of Saturn*, 4.
26 Sebald, *Vertigo*, 46.
27 W.G. Sebald, *Campo Santo*, trans. Anthea Bell (New York: The Modern Library, 2006), 3.
28 Ibid., 3–4.
29 Ibid., 5.
30 Ibid.
31 Sebald, *Austerlitz*, 120.
32 Ibid., 9.
33 Dante, *Inferno*, 3.
34 Sebald, *The Emigrants*, 156.
35 Sebald, *Vertigo*, 35.
36 Ibid., 69.
37 Ibid., 81.
38 Sebald, *Austerlitz*, 101, 117.
39 Ibid., 100–101.
40 Blanchot, *The Infinite Conversation*, 44.
41 Sebald, *Austerlitz*, 185.
42 Ibid., 95.
43 Ibid., 94.
44 Ibid., 112.
45 Rilke, *Die Gedichte*, 658; my trans.

11 Instead of concluding: Stopping

The movement of stopping

"But in the rush of everything to waste," Robert Frost reassures the newlyweds in his sonnet "The Master Speed," "That you have the power of standing still."[1] As an alternative to the "meaning of poems," Whitman proposes a similar *standing still*—perhaps in the horizontal—when he suggests that the loafer should be seduced rather than indoctrinated: "Stop this day and night with me and you shall possess the origin of all poems." The lingerer is seduced; the waiter is forced. Since one would scarcely be able to observe, from afar, the difference between seduction and manipulation, we are reminded that waiting and lingering, especially in their differences, are to some degree, but only to some degree, invisible. There is a certain intimacy, or even secrecy, that adheres to these temporalities; such is particularly the case with lingering, which might secretly turn impatience into delight.

The *origin* of all poems—just as the beginning of a single poem—is in the moment of stopping. Stopping, standing still, leaning, loafing, lingering, waiting (lingeringly), witnessing, observing, and not to forget the Whitmanesque "compassionating," these are the temporalities within which the beautiful—briefly, perhaps—reveals itself. The indescribable pause. The falling drop. The blooming hawthorns. The sun shining through the moving branches. The mallard. The moose. The *brevity* of the appearance of the beautiful is announced in the abruptness of stopping. "Suddenly I stopped," we read in Proust, "I could not move, as happens when something we see does not merely address our eyes, but requires a deeper kind of perception and possesses our entire being."[2]

In stopping, movement ceases, and yet the movement of time continues in the very ceasing. Let us call this movement whiling away, whose German equivalent is *verweilen* as we have seen in Adorno's aphorism about the Sabbath gaze. Of all the words denoting temporalities of lingering, *whiling away* seems the most serenely tranquil. The person who stops whiles away; the person who sleeps whiles away. The adverb *away*, falsely, I think, alludes to a linear passage of time; for whiling away is a duration whose temporal direction is suspended. The ideal way to appreciate a painting or a poem is to while away in it, even if one might have to be shaken out of the painting or out of the poem. The person who whiles away may fall asleep in her Sabbatical calm. If so, we might say that the degree of observable motion or movement descends from wandering, to strolling, to loafing, to lingering, to whiling away, but each of these temporalities fluidly merges into the other. The person who stops is already on her way to sleep. While she stops, she may be said to linger. Stopping initiates lingering. Lingering is an extended stopping.

Let me present the apparent paradox that stopping is a movement with the image of a boat floating in the current of a river. Because of the boat's drag, the speed of the river that flows past the boat is slightly greater than the movement of the boat. To the person in the boat, the movement of the boat is imperceptible; indeed, if she peers out of the boat into the moving stream, it appears as if she were standing still. And yet the boat moves. The movement of the boat, having seemingly stopped, is the movement of time in the aesthetic experience, a timeless stillness. Here is Marcel imagining such enchanted drifting in the Vivonne:

> How often did I see, and want to imitate, as soon as I should be at liberty to live as I chose, a rower who, having let go of his oars, had lain flat on his back, his head down, in the bottom of his boat, and allowing it to drift, seeing only the sky gliding slowly above him, bore on his face a foretaste of happiness and peace![3]

A foretaste of paradise clings to this experience; it announces itself in the slowness of the beautiful, the drifting of the boat, the gliding of the sky. The scene replays the sheer, diaphanous unfolding of the harmony of the subjective and the objective realities as Kant describes this harmony in the aesthetic experience. One might Platonize such a concept, as I have pointed out, as a fetishized unchanging timelessness, but that would precisely obscure the fact that stillness is a slowness and that stopping is a movement, and that the beautiful cannot be had, kept, and put on a shelf because it is a mere duration. When Emerson in his poem "Each and All" finds beautiful seashells and takes them home with him, he discovers that "the poor, unsightly, noisome things / Had left their beauty on the shore."[4] When Whitman leans and loafs and observes a spear of summer grass, he observes the spear of summer grass in the same temporality as his own, indeed one might say, he discovers and experiences his temporality as comparably fragile and transient, and therefore as existentially, perhaps even morally, similar. The exemplification of human transience in the fleetingness of an aesthetic moment seems, albeit unconsciously, experienced in a passage quoted earlier, when Swann feared "the slightest motion might compromise the fragile, exquisite, and supernatural magic that was so close to vanishing."[5]

The poem's stopping

The waiter who stops, stops waiting because the train has arrived, or she starts to linger because she observes a spear of summer grass. She lingers in a temporality that has slowed to a seeming stopping. The slightest motion might compromise it. She stands still. She leans slightly forward. She is passive but vigilant. She stoops over Winterson's flower bed. If she were to receive advice from the productively busy and harried, she would be told that such leaning will end in her falling—behind. But she lingers self-forgetfully; she learns the origin of all poems. She has lost her gaze in the stillness of its day of creation.

The risk of falling behind, or of falling out of sync with the busy and the harried, is the poet's professional duty and hazard at once. Stopping—of time, of intention, of purpose—is the Romantic trope *par excellence*. We find it in Wordsworth and Whitman alike. In Wordsworth programmatically, as we have seen in the lines "'I sit upon the old gray stone, / And dream my time away'";[6] or in the lines "Dull would he be of soul who could pass by / a sight so touching...."[7] The same imperative to linger, not to pass by, is addressed to the reader of "Michael" who "might pass by, / Might see and notice not...."[8] In Coleridge's "The Rime of the Ancient Mariner," the mariner stops the wedding guests and prevents them from going to a wedding feast—a frequent allegory of heaven in the Christian Bible. Many poems imply that the poet stands still, stops, lingers, and many poems thus also suggest that such stopping and lingering is contrary to all economic interest. Unlike a novel that one reads by waiting for the end of the sentence and for the end of the page, to recall Sartre, a poem is a stopping. "To read poetry," says Bachelard, "is essentially to daydream."[9] A poem, as we have seen, is not a waiting room. It is not to be passed through.

Promises

One of the most famous iterations of such stopping occurs in Frost's poem "Stopping by Woods on a Snowy Evening." "He will not see me stopping here" announces the speaker, intimating the shy illicitness of his intention to stop "Between the woods and frozen lake / The darkest evening of the year."[10] The owner of the woods, for whom the woods likely hold economic interest, might think of such stopping as pointless, unreasonable, or perhaps even as transgressive. There is, as the long, dark night in Frost's poem intimates, something risky about stopping to watch the woods fill up with snow. It might take forever. One might never keep one's promises. One might advisedly, as Frost warns in "Desert Places"—where snow and night are "falling fast"— defy the Romanic imperative and decide on "going past / ... lonely as it is."[11] There is, for different reasons, something risky about stopping this day and night with Walt Whitman. One might precisely not regret it the morning after. In "Stopping by Woods on a Snowy Evening," the horse—clearly denigrated to a workhorse—rightly "gives his harness bells a shake / To ask if there is some mistake" but neither the bells nor the clumsiness of the rhyme awaken the traveler from his trance. For there is another sound in the woods that evening; it is the sound of "the sweep / Of easy wind and downy flake" which is the outward manifestation of the traveler's mental and physical lingering.

The poem ends with the traveler's resolute determination to keep his promises. Frost does not tell us what promises these are but we can surmise that they have to do with the fulfilment of ultimate, essential obligations, perhaps no less than the fulfilment of life itself, since the traveler emphatically repeats to have "miles to go before I sleep, / And miles to go before I sleep." The repetition of that final couplet implies the arduous labor that it is to fulfil the promise of one's life. One has to stay alive for it. But that is the promise the traveler has perhaps in that long pause after "lovely, dark and deep" found in the silent falling of the snow—the promise of life that now enables him to keep his promises.[12]

If they are made out of habit, they are not promises. If they are made out of necessity, they are not promises. If they are made out of duty, they are not promises. If they are made out of fear, they are not promises. Neither habit, nor necessity, nor duty, nor fear compels the traveler to stop. The promises he intends to keep originate from a realm outside of or prior to a contractual economy. Such, too, is Benjamin's point that I quoted early on: "Empathy is possible only to the solitary; solitude, therefore, is a precondition of authentic idleness."[13] Promises, thus, if they are to have value, might most felicitously originate in the authenticity, freedom, and solitude of self-reflection, in the enchanting calm of a snowfall, in the vast space of liberty that Frost's poem presents to us as a stopping by woods on a snowy evening. A promise made from such provenance would imply a continuity of the inwardness and authenticity of character.[14]

We are not horses. "Roads are made for horses and men of business," Thoreau reminds us.[15] For Kant, the beauty of a human being is comparable to that of a horse when it implies a purpose of "what the thing ought to be."[16] In Stevens's poem "The Pure Good of Theory," "Time is a horse that runs in the heart, a horse / Without a rider on a road at night."[17] In Frost's poem, the horse impatiently waits; the traveler pleasurably lingers. Stopping, pausing, lingering, indeed reading, listening, and looking are, as we have seen, essential conditions for aesthetic and ethical insight. They are neither simplistically useful, nor immediately practical, nor always convenient, nor highly regarded by horses. "I do not say these things for a dollar or to fill up the time while I wait for a boat,"[18] Whitman proclaims. Aesthetic and ethical insight, the perception of the beautiful and of the good, is not granted to one who does not stop and risk her journey, as the poem suggests, indeed who does not risk her future.

Surely, the traveler in Frost's poem had not planned to stop, was not told, was not asked, indeed did not know she would stop. The beautiful cannot be ordered, scheduled, planned, or predicted. It befalls us like snow, like sleep. It happens in that it happens through us, if we were so inclined as to lend ourselves to its happening through our wise passivity in it. And if it is true that the kind of stopping we witness and experience in Frost's poem leads to the perception of beauty and that perception to the ability to make free moral choices—because the perception of beauty is eminently free—then stopping, too, is an activity—wisdom or vigilance turning passivity into activity. Even waiting can be an activity—*if the waiter lingers in it*. Even waiting may present itself as an opportunity to encounter those aspects of life otherwise obscured by haste. But we mostly wait in haste.

If I stop, I may find my promise and therein the power to keep promises. If I accept my experience of waiting rather than being merely subjected to it, if I resist the commercialization of time, if I own my time, if I stop to watch the woods fill up with snow, I make time matter—and then I matter. Matter, of course, is just another word for time, and time another word for being.

Silence

The evening on which the traveler stops is a vast cosmic event, regular, predictable, determined by the light and angle of the sun in relation to the tilt of the earth—what Richard Poirier in his comments on Frost's poems calls nature's "cycles or design."[19] It is time with the rhythm of a measure. The measure of this cosmic time is audible in the poem as the iambic tetrameter that runs through each line like Stevens's horse without a rider.

The traveler's stopping "To watch the woods fill up with snow" intimates a deep silence. Nowhere in the poem is the depth of this silence more audible than in the last stanza. The sleep that this traveler reminds himself to delay is already audible in the calm declarative syntax and the slow rhythm of the line "The woods are lovely"—pause—"dark and deep." Long pause. Precisely because lovely is dark and deep—"... I have promises to keep"—pause. The depth of this loveliness, dark and deep that it is, fathoms the depth of the promises.

It is in these silences or pauses or intervals where the mechanical rhythm of the tetrameter beat becomes a melody. And it is in these subtle lengthenings or hesitations of the beating and battering meter, beneath, above, or slightly outside the tetrameter, where I slightly deviate from the mechanics of the meter, it is there where I am individualized, humanized, where the poem slides its voice slightly out of the metric beat; it is there where I am spoken, and there where I make my promises. No wonder my student, asked to read the poem aloud, is shy to deviate from the mechanical meter to give voice to the melody of the poem, for she would give voice to the melody of her duration that is in the poem's sounds and intervals. If Swann had heard them, they would have opened his soul.

The tonality of the iambic terameter predominantly of dark vowels lifts sequentially, slightly to my ear, from "*woods*" to "*lovely*" to "*dark*" and at the end to the high pitch of "*deep*" that prompts the traveler's awakening, "But I have promises to *keep.*" The sequence maps the awakening of the traveler's humanity in the midst of an overwhelmingly authoritative natural rhythm. Or to say this differently, it seems an altogether Freudian sequence of associations suddenly coupling the seductive, beautiful dark and *deep* of the woods to the obligatory *keeping* of promises. Since in this stanza the sound of *sleep*, so to speak, is sustained throughout the entire quatrain, the *keeping* of promises contends with forces inviting a stopping yet deeper. It is in this liminal state between death and life, sleep and waking that we linger. It is there where Proust writes his novel. It is not least because the lingerer, the daydreamer, the loafer resemble the sleeper that they are thought to be lazy.

The ominous implications of this sleep are fortuitously resisted in "Stopping by Woods on a Snowy Evening." The beauty of the silent snowfall in the woods, like the beauty of the poem's simplicity and calm, constitute what Blanchot calls "the world which has become in me the narrowness and the limit of my repose."[20] In a narrow poem

114 *Instead of concluding: stopping*

such as Frost's—it measures but four iambic stresses in width—one sleeps with open eyes, one drifts, as Proust would say, in half-veiled thoughts, one drifts as if in a boat under the gliding sky. If the general consciousness, both socially and psychologically, does not approve of such repose, one needs *sangfroid*. A small bed such as Frost's poem, Whitman would agree, is delightfully sharable.

Notes

1 Frost, *Collected Poems, Prose, and Plays*, 273.
2 Proust, *Swann's Way*, 143.
3 Ibid., 174.
4 *Emerson's Prose and Poetry*, 432.
5 Proust, *Swann's Way*, 365.
6 Wordsworth, *The Oxford Authors*, 130.
7 Ibid., 285.
8 Ibid., 224–25.
9 Bachelard, *Poetics of Space*, 17.
10 Frost, *Collected Poems, Prose, and Plays*, 207.
11 Ibid., 269.
12 See Richard Poirier, *Robert Frost: The Work of Knowing* (New York: Oxford UP, 1977), 181; Poirier hears in that as in other poems a voice "designed to waken him into a renewed life which, unlike the life of nature, cannot depend on cycles or design, but only on will and consciousness" (180).
13 Benjamin, *The Arcades Project*, 805.
14 Cf. Ricoeur, *Memory, History, Forgetting*, where promise-making is dependent on "the sameness of character" (165).
15 Thoreau, *Walden, Civil Disobedience and Other Writings*. 231.
16 Kant, *Kritik der Urteilskraft*, § 16; my trans.
17 Wallace Stevens, *Collected Poetry and Prose* (New York: The Library of America, 1997), 289.
18 Whitman, *Complete Poetry and Collected Prose*, 243.
19 See note 12.
20 Blanchot, *The Space of Literature*, 266.

Bibliography

Adorno, Theodor W. *Minima Moralia*. Frankfurt: Suhrkamp, 1982.
Adorno, Theodor W. *Ästhetische Theorie*. Frankfurt: Suhrkamp, 1990.
Adorno, Theodor W. *Aesthetic Theory*. Trans. Robert Hullot-Kentor. Minneapolis: U of Minnesota P, 1997.
Agamben, Giorgio. *Infancy and History: The Destruction of Experience*. Trans. Liz Heron. London: Verso, 2007.
Allen, Thomas. M. Ed. *Time and Literature*. Cambridge: Cambridge UP, 2018.
Aristotle. "Metaphysics". In *Introduction to Aristotle*. Ed. Richard McKeon. New York: Modern Library, 1947.
Aristotle. "Rhetoric and Poetics". In *Introduction to Aristotle*. Ed. Richard McKeon. New York: Modern Library, 1947.
Bachelard, Gaston. *On Poetic Imagination and Reverie*. Trans. Colette Gaudin. Dallas: Spring Publications Inc., 1971.
Bachelard, Gaston. *The Poetics of Reverie*. Trans. Daniel Russell. Boston: Beacon P, 1971.
Bachelard, Gaston. *The Poetics of Space*. Trans. Maria Jolas. Boston: Beacon P, 1994.
Balsamo, Gian. "The Fiction of Marcel Proust's Autobiography." *Poetics Today* 28. 4, 2007.
Barthes, Roland. *Le Plaisir du texte*. Paris: Éditions du Seuil, 1973.
Barthes, Roland. *The Pleasure of the Text*. Trans. Richard Miller. New York: Hill and Wang, 1975.
Barthes, Roland. *Camera Lucida*. Trans. Richard Howard. New York: Hill and Wang, 1981.
Barthes, Roland. *The Grain of the Voice: Interviews 1962–1980*. Trans. Linda Coverdale. Berkeley: U of California P, 1991.
Baudrillard, Jean. "Pataphysics of the Year 2000." In *The Jean Baudrillard Reader*. Ed. Steve Redhead. New York: Columbia UP, 2008.
Beckett, Samuel. *Waiting for Godot*. London: Faber and Faber, 2006.
Benjamin, Walter. *Illuminations: Essays and Reflections*. Trans. Harry Zohn. New York: Schocken Books, 1968.

Bibliography

Benjamin, Walter. *The Arcades Project*. Trans. Howard Eiland and Kevin McLaughlin. Cambridge: The Belknap P of Harvard UP, 2003.

Berger, John. *About Looking*. New York: Vintage, 1980.

Bergson, Henri. *Key Writings*. Ed. Keith Ansell-Pearson and John Mullarkey. New York: Continuum, 2002.

Bishop, Elizabeth. *The Complete Poems*. New York: Farrar Straus and Giroux, 1992.

Blanchot, Maurice. *The Space of Literature*. Trans. Ann Smock. Lincoln: U of Nebraska P, 1982.

Blanchot, Maurice. *The Infinite Conversation*. Trans. Susan Hanson. Minneapolis: U of Minnesota P, 1993.

Bonhoeffer, Dieter. *Bonhoeffer Brevier*. Ed. Otto Dudzus. München: Kaiser Verlag, 1985.

Bonnefoy, Yves. *The Arrière-pays*. Trans. Stephen Romer. London: Seagull Books, 2012.

Boulous Walker, Michelle. *Slow Philosophy: Reading against the Institution*. London: Bloomsbury, 2018.

Bruns, Gerald L. *Maurice Blanchot: The Refusal of Philosophy*. Baltimore: Johns Hopkins UP, 1997.

Cioran, E.M. *A Short History of Decay*. Trans. Richard Howard. New York: Arcade Publishing, 1998.

Critchley, Simon. *Things Merely Are: Philosophy in the Poetry of Wallace Stevens*. London: Routledge, 2005.

Currie, Mark. "Reading in Time." In Allen, Thomas. M. Ed. *Time and Literature*. Cambridge: Cambridge UP, 2018.

The Divine Comedy of Dante Alighieri: Inferno. Trans. Allen Mandelbaum. New York: Bantam Books, 1982.

Deleuze, Gilles and Guattari, Felix. *A Thousand Plateaus: Capitalism and Schizophrenia*. Trans. Brian Massumi. Minneapolis: U of Minnesota P, 1987.

The Poems of Emily Dickinson. Ed. R.W. Franklin. Cambridge: The Belknap P of Harvard UP, 1999.

Eliot, T.S. *The Complete Poems and Plays*. London: Faber and Faber, 1985.

Emerson, Ralph Waldo. *Essays: First Series*, Vol. 2, *Collected Works*. Cambridge: Cambridge UP, 1979.

Emerson's Prose and Poetry. Ed. Joel Porte and Saundra Morris. New York: Norton, 2001.

Frost, Robert. *Collected Poems, Prose, and Plays*. New York: Library of America, 1970.

Gadamer, Hans-Georg. *Die Aktualität des Schönen*. Stuttgart: Reclam, 1977.

Gelley, Alexander. *Benjamin's Passages: Dreaming, Awakening*. New York: Fordham UP, 2015.

Gilbert, Roger. *Walks in the World: Representation and Experience in Modern American Poetry*. Princeton: Princeton UP, 1991.

Greenblatt, Stephen, Ed. *The Norton Anthology of English Literature: The Romantic Period*. New York: W.W. Norton & Company, 2006.

Han, Byung-Chul. *The Scent of Time: A Philosophical Essay on the Art of Lingering*. London: Polity P, 2017.
Hegel, G.W.F. *The Philosophy of Fine Art*. Trans. F.B. Osmaston. New York: Hacker Art, 1975.
Herrnstein Smith, Barbara. *Contingencies of Value: Alternative Perspectives for Critical Theory*. Cambridge, Mass.: Harvard UP, 1988.
Insko, Jeffrey. "Historicism." In Allen, Thomas M. Ed. *Time and Literature*. Cambridge: Cambridge UP, 2018.
Jany, Christian. "'*Das Anschauen ist eine so wunderbare Sache, von der wir noch so wenig wissen': Szenographien des Schauens beim mittleren Rilke*." *Zeitschrift für Aesthetik und Allgemeine Kunstwissenschaft* 59. 1, 2014.
Kant, Immanuel. *Kritik der Urteilskraft*. Hamburg: Verlag von Felix Meiner, 1974.
Kant, Immanuel. *Critique of Pure Reason*. Trans. Paul Guyer and Allen W. Wood. Cambridge: Cambridge UP, 1998.
Keats, John. *The Poems of John Keats*. London: Heinemann, 1978.
King, Martin Luther, Jr. *A Testament of Hope: The Essential Writings and Speeches of Martin Luther King, Jr.* New York: Harper Collins, 1991.
Kramer, Andreas. "Rilke and Modernism." In *The Cambridge Companion to Rilke*. Ed. Karen Leeder and Robert Vilain. Cambridge: Cambridge UP, 2010.
Lacan, Jacques. *Les quatre concepts fondamentaux de la psychoanalyse*. Paris: Éditions du Seuil, 1973.
Lehman, Robert. "Lingering, Pleasure, Desire, and Life in Kant's *Critique of Judgment*." *The Journal of Speculative Philosophy* 32. 2, 2018.
Levinas, Emmanuel. *Entre Nous: Thinking-of-the Other*. Trans. Michael B. Smith and Barbara Harshav. New York: Columbia UP, 1998.
Limón, Ada. *The Carrying: Poems*. Minneapolis: Milkweed Editions, 2018.
Loesberg, Johnathan. *A Return to Aesthetics*. Stanford: Stanford UP, 2005.
Lukács, Georg. *Die Theorie des Romans*. München: dtv, 2000.
Lyotard, Jean-François. *The Inhuman: Reflections on Time*. Trans. Geoffrey Bennington and Rachel Bowlby. Stanford: Stanford UP, 1991.
MacArthur, Marit. "Across the Land and into the Water." *The Yale Review* 1. 101, 2013.
Marvell, Andrew. *The Complete Poems*. Harmondsworth: Penguin Books, 1976.
Maxwell, Glyn. *On Poetry*. Cambridge: Harvard UP, 2013.
Merleau-Ponty, Maurice. *Signs*. Trans. Richard C. McCleary. Chicago: Northwestern UP, 1964.
Millier, Brett C. *Elizabeth Bishop: Life and the Memory of It*. Berkeley: U of California P. 1993.
Milton, John. *Paradise Lost*. Ed. Gordon Teskey. New York: Norton, 2005.
Nietzsche, Friedrich. *The Dawn of Day*. Trans. John F. McFarland Kennedy. New York: MacMillan, 1911.
Poirier, Richard. *Robert Frost: The Work of Knowing*. New York: Oxford UP, 1977.
Poulet, Georges. *Études sur le temps humain*. Vol. 3. Paris: Librairie Plon, 1964.

Proust, Marcel. *The Guermantes Way*. Trans. Mark Treharne. New York: Penguin Books, 2002.
Proust, Marcel. *Swann's Way*. Trans. Lydia Davis. New York: Penguin Books, 2003.
Proust, Marcel. *In the Shadow of Young Girls in Flower*. Trans. James Grieve. New York: Penguin Books, 2005.
Ricoeur, Paul. *Time and Narrative*. Trans. Kathleen Blamey and David Pellauer. Vol. 2 Chicago: U of Chicago P., 1985.
Ricoeur, Paul. *Memory, History, Forgetting*. Trans. Kathleen Blamey and David Pellauer. Chicago: U of Chicago P, 2004.
Letters of Rainer Maria Rilke: 1892–1910. Trans. Jane Bannard Greene and M.D. Herter. New York: Norton, 1972.
Rilke, Rainer Maria. *Die Gedichte*. Frankfurt am Main: Insel, 1987.
The Selected Poetry of Rainer Maria Rilke. Trans. Stephen Mitchell. New York: Vintage, 1989.
Saphire, William. "Childhood Memories." In *Others for 1919: An Anthology of the New Verse*. New York: Nicholas L. Brown, 1920.
Scherpe, Klaus R. *"Auszeit des Erzählens: W.G. Sebalds Poetik der Beschreibung."* In *Schreiben ex patria / Expatriate Writing*. Amsterdam: Quill, 2009.
Schiller, Friedrich. *"Über die Ästhetische Erziehung des Menschen."* In *Philosophische und Gemischte Schriften*. Basel: Birkhäuser Verlag, 1968.
Schlegel, Friedrich. *"Idylle über den Müßiggang."* In *Kritische Friedrich-Schlegel-Ausgabe*. Vol. 5. München: Holzinger, 1962. 25–29.
Schweizer, Harold. *On Waiting*. London: Routledge, 2008.
Schweizer, Harold. *Rarity and the Poetic: The Gesture of Small Flowers*. Basingstoke: Palgrave Macmillan, 2016.
Sebald, W.G. *The Emigrants*. Trans. Michael Hulse. New York: New Directions, 1996.
Sebald, W.G. *Die Ringe des Saturn*. Frankfurt: Fischer, 1997.
Sebald, W.G. *The Rings of Saturn*. Trans. Michael Hulse. New York: New Directions, 1998.
Sebald, W.G. *Vertigo*. Trans. Michael Hulse. New York: New Directions, 1999.
Sebald, W.G. *Campo Santo*. Trans. Anthea Bell. New York: Modern Library, 2006.
Sebald, W.G. *Austerlitz*. Trans. Anthea Bell. New York: Modern Library, 2011.
Simmel, Georg. *Philosophische Kultur*. Berlin: Verlag Klaus Wagenbach, 1986.
Steiner, Wendy. *The Scandal of Pleasure: Art in an Age of Fundamentalism*. Chicago: U of Chicago P, 1995.
Steinfeld, Thomas. *Süddeutsche Zeitung*, December 17, 2001.
Stevens, Wallace. *Collected Poetry and Prose*. New York: The Library of America, 1997.
Stewart, Susan. *Poetry and the Fate of the Senses*. Chicago: U of Chicago P, 2002.
Stewart, Susan. *The Open Studio: Essays on Art and Aesthetics*. Chicago: U of Chicago P, 2005.
Stewart, Susan. *The Poet's Freedom: A Notebook on Making*. Chicago: U of Chicago P, 2011.

Svendsen, Lars. *A Philosophy of Boredom*. Trans. John Irons. London: Reaktion Books, 2005.

Thoreau, Henry D. *Walden, Civil Disobedience and Other Writings*. New York: Norton, 2008.

Tung, Charles. M. "Technology and Time: Clocks, Time Machines, and Speculation." In Allen, Thomas. M. Ed. *Time and Literature*. Cambridge: Cambridge UP, 2018.

Wagner, Matthew. "Time and Theatre." In Allen, Thomas. M. Ed. *Time and Literature*. Cambridge: Cambridge UP, 2018.

Weil, Simone. *Waiting for God*. Trans. Emma Craufurd. New York: Perennial Classics, 2001.

West-Pavlov, Russell. *Temporalities*. London: Routledge, 2012.

Whitman, Walt. *Complete Poetry and Collected Prose*. New York: Library of America. 1982.

Williams, Raymond. *Marxism and Literature*. Oxford: Oxford UP, 1977.

Winterson, Jeanette. *Art Objects: Essays on Ecstasy and Effrontery*. London: Vintage, 1996.

Woolf, Virginia. "The Moment: Summer's Night." In *Collected Essays*. Vol. 2. New York: Harcourt Brace & World, Inc., 1967.

Woolf, Virginia. *Mrs. Dalloway*. New York: Harcourt Brace & Co., 1981.

Woolf, Virginia. *The Common Reader*. Ed. Andrew McNeillie. New York: Harcourt Brace Jovanovich, 1984.

Wordsworth, William. *William Wordsworth*. Ed. Stephen Gill. The Oxford Authors. Oxford: Oxford UP, 1988.

Zuckert, Rachel. *Kant on Beauty and Biology*. Cambridge: Cambridge UP, 2003.

Index

accident / accidental 6, 21, 67, 76–7, 95
activity 14, 15–6, 18, 26, 38, 39, 112
Adorno, Theodor x, 16, 34–6, 41–2, 50, 53, 56–7, 59, 108
aesthetic ix, 2, 13–18, 35, 42, 49–51, 53–4, 56–7, 62–3, 69, 76, 78, 81–2, 84–9, 98–9, 106, 109, 110, 112
Agamben, Giorgio 18
Aristotle ix, 10, 28, 70
attention ix, 15, 21, 29–30, 35, 56, 78, 83, 94, 101
awaken / waking 25, 53, 55, 78–82, 84, 88, 99, 111, 113

Bachelard, Gaston iii, x, 4, 8, 10, 30, 43, 58, 68–9, 85–6, 99, 102, 104, 110
Barthes, Roland x, 29, 30, 32, 36–8, 59, 62, 77–8, 98–9
Baudelaire, Charles 11, 13, 24, 53
Baudrillard, Jean 39
beautiful, the xi, 13–7, 34–5, 37, 37, 42, 49–51, 63, 66, 82, 84–6, 88, 104, 106, 108–9, 112
Beckett, Samuel 20, 30
Bellotto, Bernardo 7
Benjamin, Walter x, 3, 13, 23–4, 28–9, 53, 55, 64, 69, 75–6, 80, 90, 111
Berger, John 2, 9, 13, 20, 58, 71
Bergson, Henri ix, x, 6, 7, 10, 13, 16, 21–2, 24, 40, 41, 43, 48, 61, 63, 67–8, 72, 80, 83, 98
Bishop, Elizabeth x, 54–9, 82

Blanchot, Maurice x, 18, 32, 36, 70–1, 77–9, 82, 105, 113
Bonhoeffer, Dieter 35
Bonnefoy, Yves x, 4, 8, 9, 47
bored / boredom 4, 21, 29, 30, 36–7
Boulous Walker, Michelle x, 14, 38
brevity 6, 55, 61–2, 76, 84, 88–9, 97, 99, 108
brief 1, 5–6, 22–5, 41, 44, 51, 54–5, 61, 64, 68–9, 90, 95–6, 106, 108
Browne, Thomas 93, 96
Bruns, Gerald 32

calm 8, 15, 41–2, 62–3, 67–9, 87–9, 104, 109, 111, 113
child / children / childhood / childish i, viii, ix–xi, 2, 4, 8–10, 15–8, 30, 49, 66, 75–6, 83, 85–8, 90, 94, 96, 100, 102, 106
chronotope 69–70, 97
Cioran, E.M. x, 28–9, 34
clock (-time) viii, ix, x, 2, 5, 10, 13, 15, 32, 35, 39, 55, 61, 64–5, 69, 72, 76, 79, 87, 93, 104
Coleridge, S.T. x, 17, 31–2, 41–4, 53, 76, 110
Critchley, Simon 17, 41

Dante, Alighieri 79, 87, 103–4
daydream / daydreaming x, 1, 13, 15–17, 28, 62, 69, 79, 85, 106, 110, 113
death 5, 7–8, 18, 22, 25–6, 29, 49–50, 72, 77, 94, 98, 105, 113

Index 121

Deleuze, Gilles and Guattari, Félix 10, 48
delight / delightful 2–4, 41, 44, 56, 66, 76, 85, 100, 108, 114
Derrida, Jacques 38
Descartes, René 47
dialectic / dialectical 15, 35, 88
Dickinson, Emily 31–2, 70
disinterest 9, 14, 78
duration 5–7, 10, 13, 22, 24, 31, 39–40, 63–5, 67–70, 79–83, 89, 97–100, 106, 109, 113
durée 13, 16, 24, 50, 69, 72
dying 4, 104–5

economical / economics / economy 3, 20, 25, 28, 34–5, 48–50, 64–5, 110–1
Eliot, T.S. 2, 22–3, 31, 62
embodiment / embody 5, 6, 10, 13–5, 17, 23, 31, 40–1, 63–5, 70, 88, 97, 106
Emerson, Ralph Waldo 1–3, 13–5, 17, 31–2, 37, 39–41, 53, 57, 61, 76, 109
empathic / empathy 2–4, 15, 30, 57, 97, 111
enchanted / enchanting / enchantment viii, 8–9, 36, 53, 55, 82, 85–7, 105–6, 109, 111
endurance / endure 6–7, 22, 24–6, 30, 35, 67, 88–9, 102
eternity 7–8, 36, 41, 81, 84, 87, 104–6
ethical / ethics 2–3, 13–5, 17, 49, 57, 82, 112

Faulkner, William 11
fetish / fetishize 49, 50–1, 109
flâneur 23, 32
fleeting / fleetingness x, 6, 13, 36, 43, 50, 56, 58, 62, 75, 81, 84, 89, 105–6, 110
form (aesthetic) ix, x, 6, 14, 17, 36, 39, 41, 44, 51, 55–6, 62, 69, 72, 76, 80, 83–4, 88–9, 104–5
Freud, Sigmund / Freudian 15, 113
Frost, Robert x, 3, 17, 108, 110–12, 114

Gadamer, Hans-Georg 36, 41, 84
gaze / gazing 21–2, 30, 34–5, 42, 48, 50, 53–9, 65–6, 108, 110

general, the 34–5, 41, 48–9
Genesis viii, 29
Gilbert, Roger 47, 61
God 16–7, 28, 35, 46–7, 105
Godot 20–1, 30–1, 46
grass viii–ix, 9, 28, 32, 34–6, 46–50, 76, 109–10

Han, Byung-Chul x, 25, 29–30
happen / happening ix, 3, 6, 9, 13–4, 16, 20, 28, 35, 53–4, 57, 76, 79, 83, 96, 101, 108, 112
happiness 9, 42, 86, 109
haste x–xi, 20, 29–30, 33, 36–8, 50, 62, 94, 112
Hegel, Georg Wilhelm Friedrich 10
Heidegger, Martin x, 5, 10, 29–31, 50
Holocaust 95, 105
Husserl, Edmund 10

idle / idleness / idler ix–x, 3–4, 10, 15, 28–9, 46, 48–9, 64–6, 77–8, 111
immeasurable / immeasurably 1–2, 5, 7, 55, 62, 69, 72, 77, 84, 90, 96, 105
incomprehensible / incomprehensibility 54, 88
intimacy 22–3, 81, 94, 97, 108

Kafka, Franz 20–1, 48, 77
Kant, Immanuel / Kantian x, 5–8, 10, 13–8, 37, 49–51, 53–4, 63, 76, 78, 81–2, 88, 109, 112
Keats, John 28, 31–2, 36, 39, 78, 84
King, Jr., Martin Luther 20–1
Kristeva, Julia 10, 68

Lacan, Jacques 24, 36
laziness / lazy ix–x, 4, 15, 28–9, 79, 113
lean / leaning 9, 14–5, 17, 28, 47–9, 51, 79, 100, 108–10
Lehman, Robert 15
length 25, 36, 42, 44, 47, 55, 57, 61, 64, 69, 70, 84, 99, 113
Levinas, Emmanuel 14, 17
liberate / liberation 3, 18, 22, 39
lighten / lightness 43–4
Limón, Ada 9
literary x, 10, 32, 38–9, 41, 83, 86, 103

loaf / loafer / loafing ix, 1, 4, 9, 14, 16–8, 28, 32, 35, 46–50, 69, 78, 108–9, 113
Loesberg, Jonathan 14
look / looking (cf. gaze) 7, 17, 32, 35, 49, 53–9, 86, 98–9, 102, 105, 112
Lukács, Georg 39, 61
Lyotard, Jean-François 16, 50
lyric / lyrical 9–10, 41–3, 54, 61–2, 64–5, 69–70, 85, 88–9, 104

Mallarmée, Stéphane 57
Marvell, Andrew 22–4
Marx, Karl 16
Maxwell, Glyn 69
measure / measurement ix, 1, 5, 11, 13, 22, 55, 65, 72, 81, 96, 112, 114
melody (of duration) 6–7, 13, 67–8, 79–80, 83, 89–90, 113
mémoire (*volontaire* / *involontaire*) 11, 76, 78–9
memory (voluntary/ involuntary) viii, x, 77, 79–81, 84, 86, 89, 93, 97, 104
Merleau-Ponty, Maurice 31, 63, 82
Merwin, W.S. 100
Millier, Brett C. 57
Mitchell, Steven 4
moment 1–2, 4, 8–10, 15, 17, 37, 43, 48, 54–7, 61–2, 64–5, 68–70, 75–8, 80–2, 84–8, 90, 95–6, 99–100, 102, 104–6, 108, 110
money ix, 18, 20, 30, 43, 48, 65, 90
music / musical 7, 32, 46, 63, 68–9, 80–3, 89–90

New Critics / New Critical 43, 51
Nietzsche, Friedrich x, 21, 37–40, 43, 48, 58, 76
nothing / nothingness viii–ix, 4–7, 9, 15–7, 21, 23, 29, 31, 35, 37, 40, 43, 48, 50, 61–3, 65, 78, 82, 90, 99

painterly / painting 7, 32, 36, 69, 81, 90, 102, 105–6, 109
Paolini, Pietro 101
paradise viii, 29, 36, 41, 109
particular, the / particularity 25, 35, 38, 41, 48–9, 54, 56, 86–7, 94
passive / passivity 14–5, 28, 38, 110, 112

Penelope 10, 68
photograph / photographic 59, 96–9, 102, 104
Plato / Platonize 28, 109
play (aesthetic) 10, 13, 15–8, 37, 42, 80
pleasure xi, 15–6, 30, 37, 42, 66, 76–8, 81, 86, 89
plot 10, 61–2, 82, 85, 89, 104
poet / poetic 1, 3–4, 7–10, 14, 16–7, 22–4, 28–9, 31–2, 35–7, 41–4, 46–9, 53–9, 61, 68–71, 78, 80, 85–90, 97, 99, 103, 108–14
Poirier, Richard 112
Poulet, Georges 69
promises, the 3, 110–3
Proust, Marcel x, 4, 6–7, 9, 11, 15–6, 36, 38, 41–2, 55–6, 69, 75–80, 82–5, 87–9, 103, 108, 113–4
Prufrock 22–4, 46, 80
Punctum 59, 96
Puritan ix, 3

rarity 1, 43–4, 55
Rembrandt 102
repose 10, 14, 41, 43, 113–4
rest / restful viii, 8, 10, 14, 16–7, 34–5, 41–3, 72, 80–1, 94,
Ricoeur, Paul 65, 84
Rilke, Rainer Maria x, 4–8, 10, 16, 53–6, 58, 64, 87, 105–6
Romantic(s) ix–x, 3, 8, 15–6, 28–9, 32, 36, 53–4, 64, 84–5, 110
Rousseau, Jean-Jacques 3, 15, 66–7
Rubio, Marco 49
rush / rushing 38, 61, 85, 108

Sabbath, Sabbatical 34–5, 41–2, 56–7, 59, 96, 108–9
Scherpe, Klaus R. 94, 97
Schiller, Friedrich 16, 18
Schlegel, Friedrich 29, 64
Sebald, W.G. x, 9, 14, 36, 41, 56, 89, 93–7, 99–104, 106
shy / shyly 23, 70, 94, 111, 113
silence / silent 10, 37, 70–2, 80, 83–4, 101–2, 111–3
sleep / sleeper 1, 3, 10, 70–1, 75–6, 78–82, 103, 109, 111–4

slow / slowness viii–x, 1, 4, 6–9, 14, 17, 24, 31–3, 34–44, 48, 50, 53, 56, 58, 63–5, 67–8, 70, 72, 76–7, 83, 85–6, 93–6, 98, 9, 102, 109–10, 113
small, the / smallness 30, 42, 46, 50, 94
solitary / solitude xi, 2–4, 9, 13, 15, 38, 41, 63, 65–6, 69–70, 72, 76–7, 84–6, 96–7, 102, 105–6, 111
sonnet 9, 16–7, 36, 41, 78, 108
space / spatial 3–4, 6–8, 10, 23, 25, 29, 38–9, 43, 47, 55, 65, 69–71, 81, 83, 93, 97, 100, 105, 111
stanza viii, 3, 31, 42, 48, 56–7, 69–71, 97, 113
Steiner, Wendy 23
Steinfeld, Thomas 94
Stevens, Wallace 17, 41, 88, 112–3
Stewart, Susan 14, 16–7, 26, 29–30, 38, 69
still / stillness 8, 16, 31, 34, 41, 90, 94, 96, 106, 108–10
stop / stopping 3, 9–10, 15–8, 35, 46–7, 55, 79, 86, 88, 108–13
stroll / strolling 1, 3, 23, 32, 36, 47–8, 78, 95, 101, 109
suffer / suffering 24, 43, 57, 59, 66, 105
Svendsen, Lars 21

taste / tasting 37, 50–1, 75–8, 85, 88
temporality ix, xi, 2, 4, 7–11, 13, 15–7, 23–5, 30–2, 34, 36, 38–43, 46, 56–7, 59, 61–6, 68–70, 72, 76–7, 79, 82–5, 87, 90, 95–7, 99, 103–6, 110; of lingering 8, 10, 23, 31, 34, 68–9, 79, 85, 103; of waiting 30, 63
Thoreau, Henry D. 8, 32, 86, 112
timeless / timelessness x, 8, 16, 50, 106, 109
trauma / traumatic 67, 94–6, 102
Turner, J.M.W. 105

untimely / untimeliness ix, 9–11, 47, 55, 59, 62–3, 70, 79, 85, 103, 106

vacuum cleaner manual 39, 41
vigilance / vigilant 14–5, 38, 51, 56, 94, 110, 112
Virgil 87
vocation / vocational 16, 83, 85–6, 88

wait / waiter / waiting ix–xi, 7–8, 13, 15–6, 20–6, 30–2, 35–6, 38, 46–8, 54–5, 58, 61, 63, 66, 69, 71, 76–7, 79, 82–3, 85, 89–90, 96, 99, 105, 108, 110, 112
welder 49, 51
West-Pavlov, Russell 6, 9
whiling away ix, 8, 29, 32, 108–9
Whitman, Walt viii, x, 4, 8, 14–7, 28, 30–2, 34–6, 43, 46–51, 62, 78, 85, 105, 108–12, 114
Williams, Raymond 50
Winterson, Jeanette 33, 71–2, 76, 110
Woolf, Virginia x, 9, 36, 41, 61–2, 65, 68–71, 89
Wordsworth, William x–xi, 9, 16–7, 28, 31–2, 36, 41, 43, 53, 110

Yablon, Nick 24

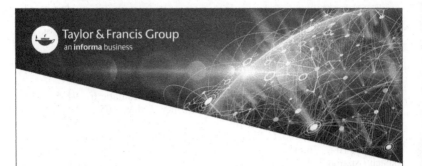